HOW TO GET OUT OF DEBT

HOW TO GET OUT OF DEBT

A Simple Biblical Approach

By

Craig Kelley

ISBN: 0615583849

ISBN-13: 978-0615583846

For Dylan, Madison, Alexandra and Emma

Contents

Purpose of the Book

How To Get Out Of Debt is a faith based approach to getting out of debt and staying out of debt. It is not about having "blind" faith but rather using a simplified system for making sound financial choices based on God's word.

The system is easy to understand and is designed to help you master money management. You don't need to be an expert or have a lot of money to get started. Because the Bible instructs us to go to the Lord in prayer for any and all things, our first activity will be prayer. So before we begin, let us pray.

Dear Lord,

Thank you for this wonderful day. Thank you for giving us another day to breathe and to praise you. Thank you for all of the marvelous gifts that you have blessed us with. Please, Lord, let us use these gifts to further your kingdom and for your glory. Help us, Lord, to remember that you are in control and that everything comes from you. We pray that you will be with us spiritually, physically and financially, Lord, and that you will bless us and expand our territory. Please reveal yourself to us so that we may become more like you.

In Jesus' name we pray,
Amen

Introduction

After many, many struggles with my finances, I decided it was time for me to put a plan in writing that I could use and revisit often. I wanted to be sure I was on the "right" track. Like any plan, I knew it would need to be updated occasionally as my life and circumstances changed. My goal was to come up with a solid foundation of Christian principles that would stand the test of time and keep me on the path to a life free from financial stress. I knew that adhering to a plan would take discipline and that there would be hills—no, make that mountains—to climb in order to reach my goal, which I call "financial freedom." I was ready though. Jesus says with the faith of a mustard seed we can say to the mountains "move" and they will move (Matthew 17:20). Move mountains? Yes. We need only the faith of a simple mustard seed. We have to let go, have faith and let God! Sound easy? It may be the hardest thing you ever do. The key word is *faith*. Every plan requires faith. Without it, you are doomed to fail. Taking the first step is an act of faith! And by reading this book, you are doing just that—taking the first step.

Pray and trust God to do the rest. He is in control. We are blessed to be given the opportunity to manage all of this fun stuff while we are in this life. Life is but a blink of an eye in the design of eternity. Make the most of each minute. Stay focused on the Eternal.

About Me

I grew up in a household where my mother worked part time as a beautician and my father struggled to keep a job for more than six months at a time. Money was always an issue and my parents' struggles were evident in their marriage. According to statistics, the number one cause of divorce is unresolved money issues. It is said that "Money makes the world go around," but it is also said that "Money is the root of all evil."

What does the Bible say about money? If we look at 1Timothy 6:10 it says:

10 For the love of money is a root of all kinds of evil. Some people, eager for money, have wandered from the faith and pierced themselves with many griefs. (NIV)

What can we take from this? Money is not the root of all evil; however, the *love* of money is a root of "all kinds of evil." Make sense? When we put our love or concern for money before our love for God, then it becomes our idol. In essence we are saying we trust in money more than we trust in God. We can make the same observation concerning water. Is water evil? Most would quickly agree no. But, like money, it depends on how it is used. Water—although it is not evil in itself—can be used for good or evil purposes. It nourishes the body and sustains us; but it can also drown us. For years, I believed that money was evil...that it was a bad thing and not good in the eyes of God. As I grew older, I struggled with this belief.

I wanted to be rich when I grew up and I felt guilty about that desire. The people who were rich I despised — mostly out of jealousy — and yet I wanted to be like them. Why? Funny enough, it wasn't because I wanted the money or to be able to buy whatever I wanted. The main reason I wanted to be rich was so that the fighting would stop. I watched from afar the families that appeared to be doing well financially and living the American dream. These appeared to be happy families with picture-perfect Christmases. In my distorted thinking, I saw these families as being more valuable to the world, whereas I was just a small, worthless poor boy. I concluded that the amount of money one made determined his or her worth as a person. I was not unique in my thinking. Unfortunately, I think most of the world has adopted this same falsehood. This may explain why everyone is now working at breakneck speeds 24/7/365 and has no time for family and God.

Another interesting statistic is that the number of people suffering from depression is at an all-time high, despite the availability of every single toy, computer, fast car, or fancy vacation we could ever want. There are so many *things* to fill our time and make us happy. *So why aren't we?*

For me, I just wanted the fighting to stop. I wanted peace. I thought money was the answer and would give me that peace of mind I longed for.

In fourth grade, I made the decision that I would go to college when I got older. Nobody in my family had ever gone to college and I was determined to start a new trend. Not only would it give me the opportunity to get ahead financially, but it would also put me in the company of a new class of friends. It was a nice dream and it gave me something to look forward to while growing up. As I progressed through my childhood, I learned a few things that changed my perception about money.

- God is GOOD.
- You can have money AND be a good, God-loving person.
- Not all people who have money are nice.
- Not all people who don't have money are nice.
- Bad guys don't always lose.
- Good guys don't always lose.
- We need to break down our muscles in order to make them stronger.

We need to break down our muscles in order to make them stronger? Yes, just like financial freedom is waiting for you on the other side of this mountain. You need to climb it to get to the other side. On the other side you may find a bigger mountain, but that's OK. God gives us small struggles so that we can be ready for the big ones, small hills so that we can eventually climb mountains, bad so that we can know the good, valleys so that we can experience the beauty at the peaks and failures so that we can savor our successes. If you have failed—like I did in the past—to get a hold on your financial situation and it has become a thorn in your side, I encourage you to take this time to pray honestly to God.

Dear Lord,

Thank you! Thank you for new beginnings. Thank you for giving me *another* chance. Lord, please be with me as I learn to manage all that you have entrusted to me, specifically my finances. I pray, Lord, for the discipline to remain steadfast in your plan and to get back up when I fall down, knowing that you are right here beside me always. Lord, more importantly, I pray that you will give me inner peace as I strive to please you. Help me, Lord, to live all of my life for you.

In Jesus' name,
Amen

Chapter I
Getting Started

Congratulations! You are taking the first step in learning how to better manage your finances. Getting started is half the battle. In this chapter we will look at your current financial situation and I will introduce you to a personal financial statement. Without the need for an accounting degree, you should be able to see where you are and what you need to improve upon. This is a critical step. You need to know where you are so that you can get direction as to where you want to be. As I mentioned before, prayer is integral to a Christian life so please take a moment and pray with me.

Dear God,

Thank You for helping me to take my first step to financial freedom and peace of mind! I am a little anxious, a little scared and yet excited to see where I stand financially. I pray, Lord, that You bless this time that I'll spend learning about my finances. Please open my mind and heart to new ideas. Lord, I know all things come from You. Give me the strength and skill to use what I have been most graciously blessed with.

Thank You, Lord,
Amen

The Personal Financial Statement (PFS)

A financial statement is a document that gives an overview of the assets, income, expenses and debts of a person or company, and is usually used by banks to assess a person or corporation's financial health. Usually, when considering lending money to a person or corporation, financiers will look at this report card—like document. A PFS can be as simple or complex as you want to make it. For our purpose, we are going to concentrate on keeping it simple so that you have a clear view of your current financial situation. There are four major components of a financial statement: (1) asset, (2) liability (debt), (3) income and (4) expense. I will explain each below.

Asset: An asset is an item of value. Assets can include cash, stock, real estate (if you are not renting), vehicles, etc. Money is a liquid asset.

Liability: A financial obligation. Any credit cards, loans, debts owed, etc. Your mortgage is a liability as is any other real estate/rental properties you may own.

Income: Any income you receive from your job, rentals properties, stocks/bonds, dividends, businesses, etc.

Expense: Any monthly living expense. This includes such items as utilities, cable, Internet service, insurance (home/life/personal/renters) and taxes (property) to name a few.

Note: If you are unsure if an item is considered an asset, liability, income or expense, e-mail me at **craig@5minaday.com** and I'll offer a suggestion as to where you could categorize it.

Asset

Now that you have a very basic knowledge of the elements of a PFS, it is time to create your very own. We'll start first by using the Asset Sheet and listing items under each category. Let's start with the Asset column. List the asset name, the value (what it is worth if you had to sell it today), how much you still owe on it (zeroes are good!), and the monthly payment. Remember, honesty is crucial to your success with your PFS.

Asset Sheet

Asset Name	Value *(if sold today)*	Loan Balance	Monthly Payment
Ex 123 Sycamore Lane	$140,000	$89,000	$684
Savings Account	$5,500	------	------
Total:			

Include any real estate that you own, vehicles, businesses (be careful not to overvalue your business), personal belongings, stocks, bonds, bank accounts, etc. Remember the value is what you could get for it today if you were to sell it. It won't help you by adding $100,000 for personal property such as furniture, clothing, etc., unless you can *honestly* sell it all today for that price. When you are finished listing all of your items total them up in the last column. There is a blank Asset Sheet in Appendix A if you need additional space. You can set this aside after you have finished it. We will use it later to compile your PFS.

Liability

Now that you have an idea of what your assets look like, let's check your liabilities next. In most cases (and hopefully), the liability will be directly linked with an asset. For our purposes, I am going to ask you to list all your liabilities—even if they are duplicated as is the mortgage, for example. Most people have a loan (liability) associated with the property (asset). By listing it in both places, you will see how it relates shortly. Now list all of your liabilities. If you need extra space, I have included a full Liability Sheet in Appendix A.

Liability Sheet

Liability Name	Loan Balance	Monthly Payment
Ex 123 Sycamore Lane	$89,000	$684
2005 Honda Civic	$4,300	$220
Total:	$93,300	$904

After you have included all of your liabilities, calculate the totals for the Loan Balance and Monthly Payment columns and enter the figures in the shaded boxes. I hope that you have more assets than liabilities, but don't worry if that's not the case. This is why we are working together. The goal is to have more assets than liabilities. We will determine your NET worth shortly by using both of these lists. This is a great way to see where you currently stand. You can set this worksheet aside for now. We will come back to this when we put our PFS together.

Income

Now we are at the income portion of your PFS. On this sheet, you will want to include any regular, recurring NET income that you receive.

NET income is what you have left after taxes, 401(k) deductions, etc. It is the face amount of the check you take to the bank.

This is a *monthly* income sheet so if you get paid weekly (52 times a year), you will want to take your annual NET salary and divide it by 12 months. If you get bonuses, do not include them. A bonus is exactly that, a bonus, not a guarantee. We want to keep our PFS as accurate and conservative as possible. Bonuses are good, but they should not be depended upon for regular living expenses. If you have rental properties, use the average monthly NET income (after ALL expenses have been paid). Factor in a vacancy rate if you have owned the property for a while and know that it applies. (For those of you who are unfamiliar with a vacancy rate, that's OK. We just want to get as close as possible.) Be sure to include any other income that you regularly receive and could cash or deposit at the bank, such as dividends, annuities, trusts, etc.

I only use NET income from paychecks and rentals even though banks often will look at your GROSS (before taxes/deductions) income. I do this because you can only cash the NET amount from your paycheck. That is the "real" number. You are deceiving yourself if you use your GROSS income.

If you are fortunate enough to need extra space, I have included a full Income Sheet in Appendix A.

Income Sheet

Income Source	Monthly *(NET)*	Yearly *(NET)*
Ex XYZ Corporation	$2,400	$28,800
Part-time painting	$500	$6,000
Total:		

Expense

Now we come to the dreaded monthly expenses. We are going to include every monthly expense you can think of. If it is an annual expense, divide it by 12 to get the monthly total. Start with your utilities and work your way down. Don't forget to include groceries and gas! You will want to include pretty much everything that you pay for out of your NET income. Do NOT include your mortgage payments or anything that you listed on the Liability Sheet. If your property taxes and homeowners insurance are not being escrowed on your mortgage payments, include them here. If you have any annual expenses, such as a life insurance policy or personal taxes, divide the total by 12 and include it here. We are looking for *all* monthly recurring expenses. Our goal is to eventually get this sheet down to as few items as possible. Don't be intimidated. Staring in the face of your monthly bills is not a fun thing to do but we are only doing it because we want to eventually bid them farewell. I had an accountant tell me often "paying taxes is a good thing. It means you are making money." Still, paying taxes is a difficult pill to swallow. If you need extra space, I have included a full Expense Sheet in Appendix A.

Expense Sheet

Expense	Monthly	Yearly
Ex Electric Service	$100	$1,200
Total:		

Congratulations! Task one is complete. For some of you this may have been more laborious than for others. However, this process is essential in order to know where you currently stand financially. If you are not the bill payer in your household then this should have been an eye-opening experience for you. You should be aware of not only how much money is coming into your life but also, and more importantly, how much money is going out and where it is going. Since all things come from God (Corinthians 8:6), it is our responsibility to manage money well.

Corinthians 8:6 (NIV)

6 yet for us there is but one God, the Father, from Whom all things came and for Whom we live; and there is but one Lord, Jesus Christ, through Whom all things came and through Whom we live.

As a parent, I love giving my children gifts. I enjoy seeing the expressions on their faces when they open them. It is a simple pleasure in my life. I would give them the world if I knew it was God's will. At the same time, when I give a gift and it is disregarded and not appreciated, my gift-giving desire wanes. I still love my children whole-heartedly, but during these times I see it may be necessary to give gifts of a different nature instead — gifts that won't become an addition to the already-high pile of yesterday's latest and greatest soon to be forgotten toys. I'm speaking of the kinds of gifts that will help them learn responsibility and thankfulness or teach them values that will stand the test of time. If I feel this way with my children, I can only imagine how God, the Father of all, who loves us at depths we are incapable of experiencing, wants to give us true blessings in our lives. Fortunate for us, we get many, many chances to learn how to use those blessings from God.

Since nobody is perfect, taking action to learn and carry out your newfound knowledge is absolutely essential. We have taken the first step in learning about our finances and now we will use the information we have gathered to assemble our very own personal financial statement. Once finished, we will be able to see where we stand at this point in time and what we need to work on to reach the road to financial freedom.

Compiling Your PFS

With your worksheets in hand (Asset, Liability, Income and Expense), we will first determine your NET Worth. Your NET Worth is what you are worth financially. It's the amount of liquid cash you would have left if you sold everything you owned and paid off all of your debts.

Simplified Personal Financial Statement

Simplified Personal Financial Statement	Date:
Total Assets Value:	$167,500
Total Liabilities Loan Balance:	$93,300
NET WORTH:	$74,200
Monthly Income:	**$2,900**
Monthly Expenses:	
Monthy CASH FLOW:	

Total Assets Value

Enter the total assets value (from the Asset Sheet) below. This is the total you get when you add up all of your assets. If you remember from above, it's the grand total that you would have if you liquefied (turned into cash) all your assets.

Asset Name	Value (if sold today)	Loan Balance	Monthly Payment
Ex 123 Sycamore Lane	$140,000	$89,000	$684
	$5,500	-	-
Personal Property	$15,000	-	-
2005 Honda Civic	$7,000	$4,300	$220
Total:	$167,500	$93,300	$904

Simplified Personal Financial Statement	Date:
Total Assets Value:	$167,500
Total Liabilities Loan Balance:	
NET WORTH:	
Monthly Income:	
Monthly Expenses:	
Monthy CASH FLOW:	

Total Liabilities Loan (Debts) Balance

Enter the total loan balance (from the Liability Sheet) below. This is the grand total that you owe on all your loans. Some of these loans may not have an asset associated with them but include the grand total for all of them anyway.

Liability Name	Loan Balance	Monthly Payment
Er. XYZ Corporation	$89,000	$684
2005 Honda Civic	$4,300	$220
Total:	**$93,300**	**$904**

Simplified Personal Financial Statement	Date:
Total Assets Value:	$167,5
Total Liabilities Loan Balance:	$93,300
NET WORTH:	
Monthly Income:	
Monthly Expenses:	
Monthy CASH FLOW:	

Determining Your NET Worth

Are you ready to see your financial worth? Whatever the result, don't be discouraged. We will work out the details on how to increase your net worth. Remember, you are worth more than anything you can buy and it is YOU whom God loves. We can do nothing to add to God's kingdom, but we can learn how to manage what we have been blessed with. All right, let's go for it. Subtract the Total Liabilities Loan Balance from Total Assets Value. Simply put, this is your NET Worth. I hope it is a positive number but it is possible that it could be negative.

If your number is above zero—congratulations! You have a positive NET Worth. If you have a negative number, we have some work to do. Again, do not get dispirited. As I said before, we will work through the details on increasing your NET Worth.

Simplified Personal Financial Statement	Date:
Total Assets Value:	$167,500
Total Liabilities Loan Balance:	$93,300
NET WORTH:	$74,200
Monthly Income:	
Monthly Expenses:	
Monthy CASH FLOW:	

Cash Flow

Now, let's see where we stand with our cash flow.

Cash flow is the money we have remaining each
month after all our bills have been paid.

Obviously, we want to have positive cash flow, i.e., more cash
coming in than going out. But in reality, it is quite possible
that you have a negative cash flow and are living on credit.
You are not alone. We will look at ways to fix that later. For
Monthly Income, enter the total under the Monthly (NET)
column from the Income Sheet.

Simplified Personal Financial Statement	Date:
Total Assets Value:	$167,500
Total Liabilities Loan Balance:	$93,300
NET WORTH:	$74,200
Monthly Income:	$2,900
Monthly Expenses:	
Monthy CASH FLOW:	

Next, for the Monthly Expenses, enter the Monthly Total from the Expense Sheet. Again, we want positive numbers, but, more important, we want honest numbers.

Simplified Personal Financial Statement		Date:
Total Assets Value:	$167,500	
Total Liabilities Loan Balance:	$93,300	
NET WORTH:	$74,200	
Monthly Income:	$2,900	
Monthly Expenses:	**$1,200**	
Monthy CASH FLOW:		

Now, subtract the Monthly Expenses from Monthly Income and enter this for Monthly CASH FLOW.

Simplified Personal Financial Statement		Date:
Total Assets Value:	$167,500	
Total Liabilities Loan Balance:	$93,300	
NET WORTH:	$74,200	
Monthly Income:	$2,900	
Monthly Expenses:	$1,200	
Monthy CASH FLOW:	**$1,700**	

How do your numbers look? If you subtracted Monthly Expenses from Monthly Income and came up with a number greater than zero, great! Congratulations! If not, great! Not great that you have a negative cash flow, but great that you now know where you are financially and you can move forward on a different road to a better, less stressful financial future.

Put today's date on your PFS and keep it in a safe place. You will need it for comparisons in a few months.

Conclusion

In this chapter, I have introduced a simple version of a personal financial statement. We learned what an asset is and that it is a good thing. Usually a debt in the form of a loan, otherwise known as a liability, is associated with an asset.

We learned that we need more assets and fewer liabilities in order to increase our net worth. A high net worth does not always equal living financially stress-free. It can, however, be used as a gauge to see if we are on the right track.

We also learned that our income needs to exceed our expenses. With income greater than expenses, we have positive cash flow. With positive cash flow we will be able to invest in additional assets, pay down our debts and build up our net worth. Most importantly, I hope we learned that God is for us and not against us (Romans 8:31). Knowing that God is here, present in this place, let us quiet our minds and take a moment to close this chapter in prayer.

Dear Lord,

Thank You for this time to learn about our finances. Thank You for this new understanding. Thank You for loving us unconditionally. Please be with us as we manage all that You have so graciously placed in our hands. Please remind us not only of Your love but also that in the big picture, our problems, financial or otherwise, are small. As we move forward please guide us so that we may experience financial freedom and be at peace. More importantly, please help us to find spiritual calmness knowing that Your love for us never wanes. Lord, give us a boost when we are climbing hills that seem too steep for us to ascend on our own.

Amen

Chapter II
Where You Stand on the Podium

As we start this chapter, I want us to reflect for a moment on the purpose of this book. My goal for this book is to equip you to live a life free from financial stress. It is to share some biblical principles regarding finances, and to introduce you to some new ideas that may be helpful in improving your current financial situation. I want you to be aware of your current financial state and to take responsibility as a Christian in maintaining and improving upon it. God wants us to flourish and have a solid foundation on which to build. With that said, we all come from differing backgrounds. We have all learned different values concerning money and thus our personal financial statements will be unique. However, we can lump our current progress into one of four categories. Before we see where yours fits, let us pray and ask for God's guidance.

Dear Lord,

Thank You for equipping us to serve You! Help us to learn from our failures and turn problems into solutions. Lord, please forgive us for mismanaging what You have blessed us with. Have mercy on us and be with us as we turn the page and begin anew. Walk with us as we continue to learn and lend us a hand when we fall. Help us to keep our focus on You always. Lord, we know that all things are possible through You.

Amen

Taking Your Place on the Podium

Grab your PFS and let's take a look at it. As I mentioned before, I believe we can lump most PFSs into one of four categories. For simplicity sake, I have labeled them Gold, Silver, Bronze and Honorable Mention. There are no losers. We are all still in the game. The goal is to move up the podiums until we reach Gold. But even when we make it there, it's not over. Platinum waits for the truly dedicated. Let's get started by defining each podium so we can see where we stand.

Gold

The criteria for standing on the Gold podium are listed below. When you reach Gold, you are managing your finances very well and you should be living a financially stress-free life. If this is where your PFS is then enjoy it! Share your experience with others. Don't stop here. Platinum is your next goal.

- Assets **are greater than** Liabilities
- Income **is greater than** Expenses

- Expenses **are less than** 65% of your NET Income.
  - Formula: (Expenses ÷ Income) x 100
- Tithing regularly
- Bank account has enough to cover 3–6 months of Expenses. (Better known as an Emergency Fund.)
- No credit card, personal loan or auto loan debt. Mortgage debt is OK as long as the value of the house is greater than the debt.

Simplified Personal Financial Statement	Date:
Total Assets Value:	$167,500
Total Liabilities Loan Balance:	$93.300
Assets Value Minus Liabilities:	$74,200
Monthly Income:	$2,900
Monthly Expenses:	$1,400
Monthy CASH FLOW:	**$1,500 (48% Expense)**

Savings Account (Cash Reserve): $7,000 (5 months expenses)

Silver

The criteria for standing on the Silver podium are listed below. When you reach Silver, you are doing very well. You have your finances under control and you are sailing along. You have a positive cash flow and your assets exceed your liabilities.

However, your expenses are above 65 percent of your income. We will work together to lower them. You should feel good at the progress you have made in getting here.

- Assets **are greater than** Liabilities
- Income **is greater than** Expenses
- Expenses **are more than** 65% of your NET Income. (This is an area for improvement!)
    - Formula: (Expenses ÷ Income) x 100
- Tithing regularly
- Bank account has enough to cover 3–6 months of Expenses. (Better known as an Emergency Fund.)

Simplified Personal Financial Statement	Date:
Total Assets Value:	$167,500
Total Liabilities Loan Balance:	$93,300
Assets Value Minus Liabilities:	$74,200
Monthly Income:	$2,900
Monthly Expenses:	$2,000
Monthy CASH FLOW:	$900 (69% Expense)

Savings Account (Cash Reserve): $7,000 (3 1/2 months expenses)

Bronze

The criteria for standing on the Bronze podium are listed below. At the Bronze level, you have a couple of areas to work on. The good thing is that your assets are greater than your liabilities. This could come in handy for improving your situation and moving up to the Silver podium. Your expenses are greater than your income. As a result, your expenses far exceed the 65 percent income cap we are trying to zone in on. This is a major problem and it needs realigned as soon as possible. Without correction, you are on a downward spiral.

- Assets **are greater than** Liabilities
- Income **is less than** Expenses (Need for immediate improvement!)

- Expenses are MORE than 65% of your NET Income. (Area for improvement!)
  - Formula: (Expenses ÷ Income) x 100
- Tithing regularly

Simplified Personal Financial Statement	Date:
Total Assets Value:	$167,500
Total Liabilities Loan Balance:	$93,300
Assets Value Minus Liabilities:	$74,200
Monthly Income:	$2,900
Monthly Expenses:	$3,000
Monthy CASH FLOW:	- $100 (103% Expense)

Savings Account (Cash Reserve): $0

Honorable Mention

The criteria for Honorable Mention are listed below. As you can see, as an Honorable Mention you are still in the game but there is a lot of room for improvement. Do not get hung up on this. Look at the situation honestly, take responsibility where appropriate and know that God will provide. Learn from past mistakes and move forward, encouraged by God's grace. As an Honorable Mention, you need to lower your expenses, increase your income, increase your assets and lower your liabilities. You need to get started and get serious immediately.

- Assets **are less than** Liabilities (Area for improvement!)
- Income **is less than** Expenses (Need for immediate improvement!)
- Expenses are MORE than 65% of your NET Income. (Area for improvement!)
  - Formula: (Expenses ÷ Income) x 100
- Tithing regularly

Simplified Personal Financial Statement	Date:
Total Assets Value:	$167,500
Total Liabilities Loan Balance:	**$170,000**
Total Assets Value:	**-$2,500**
Monthly Income:	$2,900
Monthly Expenses:	**$3,000**
Monthy CASH FLOW:	**- $100 (103% Expense)**

Savings Account (Cash Reserve): $0

On which podium do you stand?

Common Theme

You might have observed that, although some of the criteria were different, there was a common theme among each level. By changing a simple "greater than" or "less than," you were in the red (bad) or black (good). If only it were that easy to turn around our financial situations. The truth is it takes work.

With anything that is worth having there may be pain involved in attaining it. Marriage is a great example. Ask couples that have been together for 50-plus years what their secret is. They will tell you that the small struggles have made their marriage that much stronger. Instead of giving up, they fought the fight. They broke down their muscles so that the muscles would grow stronger. They climbed the hills to prepare for the mountains.

I wish I could tell you that it will be easy to move up to the next podium, but I would be deceiving you. It will take commitment on your part. You will have times when you really want to grab some fast food instead of eating in, or you'll want to buy something that you think you need right now instead of waiting for the cash to purchase it. These are the critical times when you can make some real progress or you can fall back into your old habits. Make the commitment now to yourself and to God to stand fast in the path to improving your finances. How sweet it will be when you get the Gold!

Tithing

You may have noticed that I mentioned tithing for each level above. I believe tithing is an important aspect of your financial responsibility. It is an act of faith. When you tithe, you are telling God that you know He is in control and that all things come from Him. You may argue that you have no extra money to tithe right now. My question to you is, "What if you were as wealthy as Bill Gates or Oprah?" Would it be easy for you to give away a million dollars? If it's not easy to give $10 or $100, it will definitely not be any easier to give the larger amount. Everything comes from God; we need to have the faith to let go and let God. If we look to the Bible, there are several passages on tithing; but we will look at just one for now.

Deuteronomy 14:22–23 (NIV)

22 Be sure to set aside a tenth of all that your fields produce each year. 23 Eat the tithe of your grain, new wine and oil, and the firstborn of your herds and flocks in the presence of the LORD your God at the place He will choose as a dwelling for His name, so that you may learn to revere the LORD your God always.

This passage suggests giving 10 percent of what you produce. A tithe doesn't have to be a monetary contribution, but I think it is one of the best offerings we can make. Why? Because it hits us where we feel it the most—in our pocketbooks. Unless we are spending our money for some form of entertainment, we have a hard time parting with it. We feel like we need to get something back in return. It's hard to just give money away, especially when we are trying to pay our bills down and save at the same time. Take the step of faith and start to give. It doesn't have to be 10 percent, just something. If what you are giving feels "comfortable," then maybe you should give more. I heard a story about a man who was never sure of the proper amount to give. He had a hard time parting with his money. He knew that the Lord loves a cheerful giver, but giving was difficult for him. He found a solution eventually. He fixed this by doubling the original amount he was giving. It didn't take long before he felt good about giving a bit more than he was once comfortable with. Remember, giving is an act of faith. Show God that you have that faith. At this point, I wouldn't suggest you get radical and give away your entire paycheck. Limit your tithe to 10 percent maximum for now so that you can work on improving your current financial situation.

Where Do We Go from Here?

Now that you have had a good look at your PFS, we will get into the practical details of managing your money to improve upon your current situation. Remember your Gold, Silver, Bronze or Honorable Mention level is not set in stone. Keep this in mind as we look at examples for these different positions. Most people learn best by example so I'll try to include as many as possible. Our next topic will be focused on income. As we close this chapter, let us pray.

Dear Lord,

Thank You for this benchmark. We now know where we are financially. We will trust in You to guide us in the right direction. Lord, please accept our gifts to You as a reminder that all things come from You, just as we once came from and will return someday. Continue to help us with the small struggles that seem so big at times. Lord, please continue to bless us as we walk with You and make the commitment to be more responsible in our financial lives.

Amen

Chapter III

Incoming–Your Income; What's Coming In

Our paycheck is the driving force of our finances. It is our reward for the 40-plus hours of hard work given each week. It never seems like enough though. If only we could earn an extra $5,000 a year, no $10,000, no, make that $20,000, then we would be set...or so we think. Although the extra income might help, the truth is that in most cases we would be standing on the same podium. Our Bronze PFS would still be Bronze, but with bigger numbers. The percentages probably would not change much. If we have a hard time managing $10 we will have a difficult or maybe even harder time trying to manage $10,000,000.

We hear all the time about people winning the lottery. They go from broke—a zero net worth—to millionaire status overnight. It would appear that their problems are over. No more financial worries and life will be smooth sailing. Then what happens? Less than two years later they are broke again and actually may be worse off financially than before they won the lottery. Instead of solving their problems, winning the lottery actually opened up a can of worms and created *more* problems. The lesson here is that money does not solve all of our problems and chances are we probably do not need more of it. We just need to learn how to manage what we have been blessed with. Let's learn how to take our first step before we start running; learn how to manage a little so that we are prepared to manage a lot.

Dear Lord,

As we continue to learn about our money and our finances, please guide us and be with us so that we keep our hearts and minds focused on you. Lord, we know that only You can give us true peace of mind and that no dollar amount would ever satisfy our soul. Help us to retain what we learn and put it to daily use in our lives so that we can reaffirm our commitment of responsibility with our finances and our commitment to You.

Amen

Types of Income

While the Internal Revenue Service lists over 30 types of income (see Appendix B), we will look at just two: "Passive" and "Earned" income. Both are good. As we probe each of these, I will offer some ideas on how to increase the flow of each one. I will also explain my philosophy regarding retirement.

Retirement? Yes, retirement. I am not a believer in the traditional definition of retirement as you will see shortly. Remember, we are learning to manage our finances not just for the present but also as a habit that we carry into the future.

Earned Income

Earned income is any income that you have to work for in order to receive. You need to put your hours in at work in order to collect this type of income. If you do not work, you do not get paid. It is what you earn from your job. You do not receive earned income unless you show up to do your job. Earned income is a result of offering your time for a service. We only have so many hours in a day so our earned income has its limits.

Passive Income

Passive income is money we receive from rental properties, business investments, dividends, interest, and anything else that we do not have to spend our time actively working for in order to receive it. We do not have to show up for these checks to be sent to us. It is having our money work for us.

Dividends and interest checks are great examples of this. You put money in an interest bearing account at the bank and you earn interest. You are doing nothing to earn that money. Your money is working for you. If you are a sole proprietor of a business you are working for Earned income.

On the other hand, if you invest in a business that does not require your involvement to run the business, then you receive Passive income from this. Real estate can be both Passive and Earned income. If you have a property management company taking care of your properties and you receive the profit checks at the end of the month, this is Passive income. If you are managing the properties then you are getting paid Earned income.

As a side note, a great thing about real estate is that in a lot of cases you can manage properties yourself with very little effort, allowing you to increase your Earned income without investing a lot of your time. We will get into real estate investing a little later in the book.

The main thing to remember is that there are two main types of income: Earned and Passive. Each one is good and can be used to improve your current financial situation.

Earned income →

You **work for money.**

Passive income →

Money **works for you.**

Experts will tell you that you should strive to have more Passive income than Earned income and that is a great idea. The more money you have working for you means the less you have to work for money and the more time you have to pursue your true passions.

Now let us take a moment to see what the Bible has to say about Earned and Passive income if it does indeed hit on the topic.

Relating This to the Bible

Let us take a look at the following passages.

Colossians 3:23–24 (NIV)

23 Whatever you do, work at it with all of your heart, as working for the Lord, not for men, 24 since you know that you will receive an inheritance from the Lord as a reward. It is the Lord Christ you are serving.

2 Thessalonians 3:10 (NIV)

10 For even when we were with you, we gave you this rule: "If a man will not work, he shall not eat."

What can we take from these passages? God is commanding us to work. He is not saying, "Build up your Passive income so that you can lounge around and no longer contribute to society." He is saying that whatever we do, do it whole-heartedly for Him, not men. Go the extra mile. Make the extra sacrifice. Passive income is good but it is not our ticket to forget our real purpose in this life.

My Personal Revelation

As a consultant, I was used to moving from client to client. I would go do my job at a company and then move on. My typical stay would be a maximum of six months. At one of my assignments, I saw six months come and go. Before I knew it, six years had gone by. I was into the same project for more than six years.

My personality is such that I require variety in my jobs, and after spending six years in one job it was starting to wear me down. Going to work started to become just that—work. As the days progressed, I felt like I was serving a prison sentence and that I would never make it to parole.

I was grateful that I was earning a living to support my family, but I was burnt out dealing with the same people every day. Most of the people in my office had a negative outlook on life. I had always heard while growing up that we were to be servants for the Lord. I took that to mean that we were all to be pastors or missionaries or be constantly preaching the gospel.

Part of me felt guilty that I did not serve in this capacity and had no desire to do so. I was never comfortable with just coming out and talking to people about God, since I always felt like I did not know enough in case they would happen to question me. I had a lack of faith. It was at this low point in my career when I finally got it. The light came on. I understood what it meant to be a servant of the Lord. I realized that my purpose for consulting was not to work for men on this project or that project but, instead, to dedicate all of my work for God. I did not have to have all the answers.

As I looked back on my career and life, I noticed that there was never really a time to worry. I should have just had faith and enjoyed every moment. We do not know what is around the next turn or how long we will be in our current job or situation *or this life for that matter.*

We need to have faith in God and trust that good things are waiting for us in the future. We need to keep a positive outlook. *I finally got it.* Matthew 6:24–26 confirms this point.

Matthew 6:24–26 (NIV)

25 Therefore I tell you, do not worry about your life, what you will eat or drink; or about your body, what you will wear. Is not life more important than food, and the body more important than clothes? 26 Look at the birds of the air; they do not sow or reap or store away in barns, and yet your heavenly Father feeds them. Are you not much more valuable than they?

I was hit with a ton of bricks when I reflected on this. Once I realized I had been trying to please people instead of God, I did a 180-degree turnaround. I decided that I would show the depressed and perpetually negative people I worked with the light of the Lord. I learned everyone's name and each time I passed a colleague, I would smile and say "hello." Not an easy task when you are in a corporate environment and see most of the people in passing only. Months later, amazingly, I was greeted with lots of genuine smiles in return. People started calling me by my name. I no longer dreaded going to work. I singlehandedly, just by changing my attitude, changed the environment in which I had to spend 40-plus hours a week. My work ethic improved as well. In doing my job, I would make the extra effort because I was not simply working for a client. *I was working for the Lord.* This is a lesson that I have applied to every area of my life.

While one of our goals is to continually work at increasing our passive income, we must not forget that we are also called to do real earned income work as well. Eventually, when our passive income exceeds our monthly expenses we will have the freedom to choose what type of work we want to do. We may be able to replace our earned income with charity work instead. The bottom line is we need to keep moving forward and remain active.

Retirement

I want to mention retirement mainly because anyone who has a job will be required to think about it at some point. Most people share the same traditional definition of retirement: the carrot at the end of the stick. And we all look forward to retirement because it is the day that we no longer *have* to go to work and be at someone else's beck and call. It is that magical day when we will rest lazily in the sun and enjoy the sunrise on the golf course.

Retirement is when we will travel to exotic places and start writing the novel we have always dreamed of writing. It is when everything will slow down and we will finally have the extra time to volunteer down at the soup kitchen or the rescue mission. It may mean finally being able to start our own businesses. Whatever *your* vision for retirement, it is pretty much a safe bet that it is depicted like heaven on earth. Sure enough, retirement will be an exciting time that will be full of renewed desires to live.

My definition of retirement is slightly different. I, personally, do not want to be older when I retire. I want to be young and full of energy. I do not want retirement to mark the last chapter of my life. Instead I want it to be the start of a brand new chapter in the book of my life, and I want that chapter closer to the middle of the book, not at the end. Thankfully, my idea of retirement is possible for you *if* your PFS matches this formula.

Retirement = Passive Income > Expenses

(Translation: **Retirement** is attainable when your **Passive Income** is greater than your **Expenses.**)

In order to get to this point we will need to either increase our passive income or decrease our expenses. We most likely will need to do both. The reason retirement is traditionally at the end of the "book" is because it is not until late in life that we are able to collect social security and use our retirement savings without penalty. By then our mortgage is likely paid off and we finally have passive income that exceeds our expenses. Our passive income replaces our earned income. Even if you stay on that traditional path, it will benefit you greatly to add extra passive income starting as soon as possible. Let's look at a few ways that we can increase our passive income.

Business Investments

Investing in a Business

With any investment, there is a level of risk involved. When you invest in a business you are taking a risk. The business could fail or succeed. According to most statistics, most businesses fail within the first five years and then nine out of 10 fail within 10 years. Those odds are not good. So, you'll need to make a few sound judgments to minimize the risk involved. I would not recommend investing in a business that you are not familiar with. Know what you are getting into and think it through entirely.

The three basic key factors in analyzing a business investment are:

- **Market for business** – Does the business have enough of a demand to succeed? Can you picture this business around in five or 10 years?
- **Financial statement** – This is the report card for the business. How is it doing financially? Is it showing a profit? Are the salaries top-heavy? Is more money

going out than coming in? Before investing, do a PFS on the company to analyze its viability.

- **Competition** – What kind of competition are you up against? Is the company bleeding-edge (continually coming up with innovative products) or eating its competition's dirt (late to the table)?

Business investments are not for everyone and you will know in your heart if you have the skills or mind-set for it. Ignorance is no excuse, however. You should not discount a business proposition just because it is out of your comfort zone. In any case, I would highly recommend reading extensively on investing in businesses, talking to others who have invested, and doing your homework on any company in which you are considering investing in. Know what your involvement will be as well. Will this be a true passive income opportunity or are you going to have to put your time in as well? Investing in a vending machine business can be profitable; however, if you are doing the work your income is earned income rather than passive income.

Starting Your Own Business

Another option is to start your own business. You do not have to be a business expert to start a business, but you should have some basic business skills. There are plenty of courses and books available on starting your own business. I just want to introduce the idea that there are plenty of ways to earn extra income that do not take a large amount of your time. Starting a business will usually start out as an earned income situation. As you become established, you may be able to delegate the workload and eventually move entirely into a passive role.

The purpose of a business is to find a need and fill it.

Success Story

By now, everyone has heard of Crocs™. Crocs are not just crocodiles anymore. They are shoes that can be found in practically every household in America. Shortly after Crocs hit the marketplace, the demand exploded. Millions of these shoes have been sold all over the world.

After purchasing Crocs for her family, a stay-at-home mom decided one day to dress up the shoes by putting rhinestones in the holes. She essentially accessorized the Crocs. Her husband saw an opportunity and they jumped on it. They began selling these accessories and eventually used some equity from their home to further finance the business. Within six months, the business sold more than $200,000 worth of products. Within a year, it had sold over 2.2 million dollars worth! Shortly thereafter, the business was sold to Crocs for *$10 MILLION!* This husband and wife team is set to get another $10 million if sales targets are reached. WOW!

This story is inspiring for several reasons. First, the stay-at-home mom piggybacked on a product that already existed and was firmly entrenched in the market. Can you think of something you use every day that could be improved upon or accessorized like this? Have you seen this done with IPod accessories? Second, this company was started by a stay-at-home mom. Not a marketing research group or some high-paid consultants. It was conceived by someone just like you and me. We are all special and have great ideas! The third and final thing I want to mention about this story is the timetable. With some luck and demand already in place, the husband and wife team was able to grow this business very, very quickly.

Exercise

To get the ball rolling, let's brainstorm. Think of five things that would make your life easier. Money is not allowed to be one of the five. Think of solutions to problems rather than things you can currently buy.

For example:

> **Problem:** I need to get up from the sofa and walk to the TV to change the channel.
>
> **Solution:** I'll create a remote control device that can change the channel from where I'm sitting.

The idea here is to come up with *new* inventions or solutions to existing problems.

1.

2.

3.

4.

5.

Real Estate

I would like to start by saying that this may not be the thing for you. Just like businesses are not for certain people, the same is true for real estate. There is risk involved and you need to do your homework when investing. Unlike the stay-at-home mom's overnight success story we just read about, real estate is typically an investment where you will see increased gains over the long haul of owning the property. Since we are trying to increase our passive income, we need to make sure that whatever property we invest in will show a positive cash flow from day one. That is, after all expenses (mortgage, taxes, insurance, maintenance, etc.) we will still get a check at the end of the month. Specifically at the end of the *first* month. Not four years down the road. From day one.

For real estate to be passive income, you will need to have someone else perform the property management. Many real estate agents are also in the business of managing properties but, typically, they will just find tenants for you and then take one month's rent as a fee. A true property management company will find tenants and handle the day-to-day operations. They will fix a toilet if it needs fixed in the middle of the night. Of course, they take the fee right out of your rent but at least you are completely hands off with the property. Your profit might be lower than if you managed the properties yourself, but at the same time you are not limited on the number of units you can own. If you manage your own properties (earned income), you will reach a ceiling where you will either have to stop buying more or you'll have to call someone in to help with the day-to-day operations.

When buying real estate consider the following:

- **Location** – Will it be hard to find tenants for the house because of the location? Is the property in a safe neighborhood? What are the neighbors like?
- **Price** – Will the rent support the mortgage/taxes/insurance/etc., and still turn a profit?

- **Condition** – Do you see any repairs, minor or major, that will need to be made on the house? A house inspector can help with determining where any repairs may be necessary. If you aren't skilled in home repair (and even if you are), it would be a good idea to get a home inspector to examine the property before you buy. An extra set of eyes is always good and can give you peace of mind.

Most first-time real estate investors make the mistake of not budgeting for unforeseeable expenses. It is always the miscellaneous expenses that get you. The rule I personally follow is that I like to see a profit of at least $100 each month from each property. I like to put at least $1,000 in the bank before I take any cash flow from a property. (See Figure 1 below.) As you buy several properties and use this same approach, you accumulate a nice reserve. If you follow this rule, you are ready for the expense of replacing a furnace or hot water heater should either break down.

Rental Property Repair Reserves

Property #1 Reserve: $1,000

Property #2 Reserve: $1,000

Property #3 Reserve: $1,000

Property #4 Reserve: $1,000

Property #5 Reserve: $1,000

Property #6 Reserve: $1,000

Total available if needed: $6,000

Figure 1

Conclusion

You can choose to invest in businesses, real estate or something entirely different. There is a lot of opportunity out there. It may just take a little time to find exactly what you are looking for so be patient. You may find it more comfortable to get a part-time job instead. That is fine too. Since we are trying to increase your passive income, you would want to invest any earned income in an interest bearing account. IRAs are great for this and we will get into these a bit later in the book.

The bottom line is this: If you want to live a financially stress-free life you will need to take the steps to increase your income or lower your expenses. The more passive income you have the better. The lower the expenses you have the better. The more faith you have in God to guide you—even better. Next, we will analyze your expenses and see if we can lower or completely eliminate as many of them as possible.

Dear Lord,

Thank You for my job! Thank You for my ability to work. Thank You for the desire to work. Lord, You call us to work; work not only for our employers and clients but most importantly for You. Help us to do the best we can do at our jobs and prosper us. God, help us to stretch our comfort zones and to put our total faith in You knowing that although the things of this earth will come and go, You will remain for eternity.

In Jesus' name,

Amen

Chapter IV
Outgoing–Your Expenses

Our financial situation, at times, does not seem fair. Our incomes either stay the same or barely increase (and often decrease), but expenses always are always on the rise. Companies are becoming savvier at raising the prices and shrinking the packaging without making it noticeable to the consumer. Ask the grocery shopper in your household and he or she will tell you how this works and how common it is. Just the other week, I went to the grocery store and saw a deal on cases of soft drink. First, have you noticed that a case is only 12 cans now? Remember when a case used to be 24 cans? Now, if you want 24 cans, you have to purchase a "cube." I am still trying to get used to calling a half-case a case. The deal of the week was four "cases" for $11. That is $2.75 per case. A couple of months ago you could get four cases for $10 ($2.50 per case). Not long before that you could get five cases for $10. A quarter here, fifty cents there, who notices? But it all adds up!

Recently, in my hometown, the borough manager announced that the borough would not be raising property taxes. Great! OK, what's the catch? Well, instead of raising property taxes, the borough will be raising our water/sewer and trash bills. Wow! Let me guess, by shifting this expense the revenue will actually increase? As borough residents, we are forced to buy specially marked borough trash bags in which to place our trash for curb pickup. The most recent cost was $3 per bag. That was increased to $4 per bag. That is a 33 percent increase! When is the last time you received a 33 percent raise? The worst part of borough's plan is that it puts the entire burden on borough residents only. The residents that live on the outskirts of town, without water/sewer service/trash bag requirements, are not affected except for the fact that they will not see property taxes increase. Good for them, bad for the borough residents!

The point is we cannot control all of our expenses. Everyday living expenses keep going up. That makes getting control of our unnecessary bills even more crucial. In this chapter, we are going to take a good look at your expenses and see how we can improve your current situation.

Dear Lord,

Thank You for being with us as we look at an often frustrating area of our lives—our bills. Please be with us when we feel overwhelmed with our debt. Lord, help us to stay focused on You knowing that You paid the ultimate price so that we can be debt-free for eternity. Give us the vision to see beyond the horizon where our stress is gone and we are at peace with You. Let us look at our expenses honestly, Lord, and remain steadfast in our commitment to improve our current financial situation. Thank You for breath. Thank You for life. Thank You for Your grace.

Amen

Analyzing Your Expenses from Your PFS

You will need your Expense Sheet that you put together in Chapter I. We are going to go through the expenses on your sheet and I will give you some general guidelines on determining the difference between a necessary expense and an unnecessary expense. You may be surprised to learn that many of what you think are necessities are really desires—or as I call them "wants." Once we get a grip on differentiating between the two, you will have a much better grip on your expenses and finances overall. It is the "wants" that negatively impact your budget the most.

Needs (Necessary Expense)

A "need" is an expense that you cannot go without. It is the water/sewer and trash bill that was raised recently in my hometown. It is any expense that allows you to live a minimum lifestyle. Count your mortgage or rent as a necessary expense because if you are on your own you cannot live for free. Needs also include anything that is associated with the mortgage, such as taxes and insurance.

Essentials:

1. Mortgage/Rent *
2. Property Taxes (if you own your home)
3. Homeowners/Renters Insurance *
4. Electric
5. Gas (propane/natural)
6. Oil
7. Water/Sewer
8. Groceries *
9. Home Owners Association Fees (if you own and have to pay these)*
10. Insurance – Health/Life/Auto *
11. Prescription Medicines

Bonuses:

1. Telephone *

As you can see, a need is something that you cannot survive without. There are a few exceptions. Needs can be broken down into a few basics groups.

- Housing

- Electricity
- Heat
- Water/Sewer
- Food
- Health

Notice that I listed the telephone under bonuses. You could survive without it. When you take a moment and think of living life without a telephone for a while, you soon appreciate the luxury it offers. Our ancestors would tell us that electricity and water/sewer are luxuries as well! The truth is, we want to be financially free without pretending we are living in the past. We want financial freedom in this modern age. Understanding what our core needs are will help.

*The items that include an asterisk are expenses that you may have some control over. These are items that you can target to lower, within your essential expenses list. For example, do you really need the package deal for your telephone? Why do we need to know who is calling us? Isn't it fun to answer not knowing who is on the other end? I would venture to guess that 98 percent of the people that call you are friends and family anyway. Another feature is call waiting. Do we really need this service? Maybe my household is different than most but we rarely get an urgent phone call that needs to be answered the second the telephone rings. My point is that if we examine closely, we can find ways to lower these necessary bills. Make a note of these and think of ways to get a better grip on them.

In the next chapter, we will look at how our expenses relate with the overall picture of our budget. When I say "budget" I do not mean in the common understanding of the term. We are not going to create a plan in which we hold X amount of dollars for the electric bill, X amount of dollars for your grocery bill and so on. That is too time consuming and is very hard to turn into a habit. (For your information, experts say it takes 21 days to break or make a habit.) We will look at the overall picture of your finances and try to establish some basic rules that with little effort you can use on a daily basis.

For now, understand that these essential needs should not account for more than 65 percent of your NET income. Again, for clarification, *NET* income. That is, your income after taxes; the face value of your check you deposit (or cash) at the bank. You cannot spend your gross income so we only deal with income in terms of NET. I hope that your expenses account for a lot less than 65 percent of your NET income, but if they are above that percentage we will look at ways in which we can reduce this as well.

To the surprise of many, we have come to rely on a lot of luxury items as if they are a necessity. For example, how many houses do *not* have cable or satellite TV? Not many! TV is not a necessity. Is that hard for you to swallow? For some, I am sure that it is. I am not trying to tell you that you should or should not have a TV. I am trying to get you to open your mind and see the difference between true wants and needs. Once we get a good grasp on this concept we will be able to make better judgments when we spend, in many cases, our hard-earned money.

My Short Story

My family recently moved into a new house. Of course, when I say new, I don't mean brand-spanking newly built. Our new house is more than 30 years old. Since all of our prior houses were more than 80 years old, this house seems "new" to us.

We bought our house from an older couple who had lived in it since it was built. They had a TV. A small old, maybe color, TV. While we were viewing the house prior to buying it, I did not notice if they had TV cable, but I did notice that they did not have a satellite hooked up.

When we moved in, we placed all the furniture where we thought it should go. The next item that came off the truck was the TV. "Where should we put it?" we wondered. Naturally, we chose to put it where the TV cable outlet was located. Upon further investigation, we found that the previous owners did not have cable installed. They did not even have the line coming to the house. So for the time being we would have to go without watching our favorite shows and sporting events on TV. Believe me when I tell you I even tried the rabbit ears with several wire coat hangers dangling in different directions in order to get reception. I got nothing but a closet full of winter coats lying on the floor!

It turns out that it took six months for the local cable company to finally get the line run to the house. You heard me right. SIX months! But it was a blessing in disguise. Our children played outside more than they had ever done in the past. They rode their bikes, played on the swing set, played hide-and-seek and were constantly on the move enjoying the outdoors. They even enjoyed playing in the rain! We cooked marshmallows over a fire, took walks, read books and worked in the yard. It was adventurous and refreshing.

It was October when our cable was finally installed. Since then we have enjoyed watching the TV during the winter months but, thanks to the slowness of our local cable company, we have started a new tradition. We go without TV, except for an occasional DVD movie, from late spring to late fall. Try it yourself! Maybe you'll decide to go the whole year!

If you are like me, then you do not like to wait. With the arrival of the Internet, stores are open every minute of the year. The shipping companies have become so efficient that you can order something in the afternoon and have it on your doorstep the following day, even if it is coming from two states away. Businesses have impressively kept up with the demand for the I-want-it-now mentality. Unfortunately, this kind of mind-set has driven many families deep into debt. Someone I once worked for told me what her father used to tell her when she was a little girl. "For buy: waste time; for free: take." Every time I go to buy something, I try to remember this little saying. Most of the time, as a day or two passes by, I will usually forget all about what I thought I needed.

Below I have listed some common expenses that are really wants. Some may argue that they need these items in order to survive, but I am sure if you really sit back and look at these honestly you will agree they are luxury items (unless they in some way yield income, e.g., an instrument would be a necessity if you are a musician in a band that gets paid to perform).

Wants (Unnecessary Expense)
1. Car (with payments)
2. Cable/Satellite TV
3. Personal Care
4. Cell Phones
5. Sporting Events
6. Dining Out
7. Vacations/Trips
8. Scrapbooking
9. Music CDs/Instruments
10. Home Improvements
11. Fashion Clothing and Jewelry
12. Toys
13. Extra-Curricular Activities
14. Gifts

15. Children Investment Accounts

16. Computers

17. Magazine Subscriptions

Look at the expenses on your sheet from Chapter I. Separate the needs from the wants based on the lists above. Which list is longer? I will honestly tell you that my want list is longer. That is OK. We can have as many wants on our lists as our hearts desire, but it will need to fit into our plan. We will learn some techniques for managing our money to pay for the needs and wants. It goes without saying that the needs should come first. You would be surprised how many people neglect the needs and then find themselves in trouble. Before long, the bank or landlord is knocking on the door looking for payment for the most basic need of all, housing. And once you get behind on your rent or mortgage, it is extremely hard to get back on top of it. God calls us to pay our bills. He also calls us to not live in excess. It is our responsibility. We need to make a commitment to manage our finances more efficiently and dutifully.

Good Debt versus Bad Debt

While most people think that all debt is bad debt, I would like to offer an alternative view on this subject. Debts come in all sizes and varieties—a credit card balance, car loan, loan from your mom or dad, a mortgage, a home equity loan, a personal loan, etc. You get the idea. It is a sum of money that we owe. It could have been for a service or a thing. (If it was a "thing," most likely the excitement over the purchase is long gone and all you are left with is the debt!) Cars have a wonderful way of being overly exciting for a few months and then the idea and process of paying for them kicks in. Car loans are a great example of bad debt. What about a boat? Have you heard what they say about boats? The best thing about owning a boat is selling it…

Bad Debt: Any debt that does not make you money.

Like I mentioned, a car loan is a perfect example of this. You will rarely make money in the process of getting loans for cars. (I only say "rarely" because you may be able to turn a few dollars by selling some kind of specialty car.) I am not saying that you should not get a loan to buy a vehicle, most people have no choice in the matter. But it's best if you can pay cash. Even if you only pay half in cash, that is still better than financing all of it. Cars are so cool and fun but they cost us a lot. If I could change one thing about my own financial situation, it would be the amount of money I wasted when buying cars. As you'll read below, I learned the hard way!

My Car Story

I have not been perfect when it comes to choosing and buying cars. I bought a beautiful Audi TT Coupe. It was my first time ever buying a brand-spanking-new car. It had nice smelling leather seats, a sweet Bose sound system and drove incredibly well. I put $10,000 down when I bought the car. The car was not cheap. My price was $34,500. Wow, that is a lot of money! I bought my first rental property for less than that! So after they added all of my taxes, fees, etc., into the deal, I drove away with a shiny new car worth about $28,000 and a loan for about $27,900. What? After paying all the fees, along with the instant depreciation of the car's value, I basically gave away $10,000 to get that car. Instant depreciation is what happens when you drive your car off the dealer's lot. You lose about 20 percent when you leave with your car. That is one reason why buying from a personal seller will usually get you a better price. The price is missing the dealer's markup. Of course, you are not getting a garage/dealership standing behind your car when you buy it privately, so both may have their advantages. To make a long story short, I threw a lot of money away to get this car and in the end I had a nice car and a bad debt. When making car purchases be sure that your monthly expenses do not exceed the 65 percent ceiling we need to shoot for.

Contrary to the opinions of many, I believe that your mortgage is also a bad debt. It falls into my definition of bad debt because your house does not make you money. Before you start screaming obscenities at me, you should know that I am all for home ownership. There are many, many benefits of owning your own home. The positives far outweigh any of the negatives. The point to think about is that the mortgage can eat up a large chunk of your income. You do not make money on it. It takes away from your monthly cash flow. Usually, a house is a long-term investment. If you profit from your house it is usually years down the road. In recent times in thriving areas people have proven this wrong by "flipping" houses. That is, they will buy and sell them quickly. It is expensive to deal houses like this so you need to make a huge profit in order to make it worthwhile. I would not recommend it. The risks are high and the return on your money is not guaranteed.

In conclusion, a bad debt is a debt that does not make you money. It takes away from your monthly income. Bad debts take away from the income that you could invest, save or tithe. All bad debts plus monthly expenses should not exceed 65 percent of your monthly NET income.

Good Debt: A debt that makes you money.

A good debt will make you money. How can a debt be good? Most people would argue that ALL debt is bad. It would be great to be debt-free wouldn't it? What if someone allowed you to use their money so that you could make money? A perfect example of a good debt is a mortgage for a rental property. Wait, I just said that a mortgage was a bad debt. How can it now be a good debt? The reason is because you are actually making money by having the debt. If someone offered you $2,000,000 in properties that carried $1,000,000 in mortgages and a monthly cash flow of $10,000, would you take them? You would? Wait a minute, you would be $1,000,000 dollars in debt! It is good debt so you would be correct in accepting such a burden. I use the word "burden" sarcastically.

A business loan can also be a form of a good debt provided you are making money in the business. The thing to keep in mind is that not all debt is bad. Do not be afraid to use other people's money. The bank makes money on the interest, you make money on the cash flow and the consumer is getting a nice product or service.

Understanding Cash Flow

For some of you the term "cash flow" may be a new term. You have probably heard it as a buzzword on a get-rich-quick infomercial or elsewhere. For others, you are already familiar with the term. I would like to give you a very basic overview on cash flow and how it relates to your financial situation.

Cash Flow: The amount of money remaining at the end of the month after all expenses have been paid.

Sounds simple, right? One of our goals is to increase your cash flow. With your increased cash flow you will be able to pay down your debts, invest for the future and enjoy a treat for yourself without feeling guilty.

Take out your PFS again. Where did you fall on the podium earlier? Chances are that if you were Gold or Silver, you have a nice cash flow at the end of the month. For the Bronze and Honorable Mention contenders, we have some work to do. If your monthly expenses exceed your monthly income, you have a negative cash flow. Until the problem is corrected you will dig deeper and deeper into debt. If you are Bronze or Honorable Mention, you probably have some bad debts that we can work on paying down in order to increase your monthly cash flow. In the next chapter we will see how you can KO (knock out) your debt and free up some of your income. As I said early on in this book, becoming financially free is not easy and it takes hard work and dedication. You need to change your way of thinking. You will need to change your habits. This is not easy. All of your life you have been programmed to think the way you do today. It is time to trust God, be disciplined and be willing to change. It may mean sacrificing and not being a part of the crowd. It may hurt and you may feel sad. You will need to remain focused on the big picture. All things will come and go but in the end God will still be standing. Let us not worry about life's little details and how we feel at the moment. Be strong, knowing that God loves you and will love you if you are poor or rich. He's after your heart not your pocketbook.

Conclusion

In this chapter, we looked at our expenses from a few different angles. We took an honest look at our monthly expenses and how we define our true needs versus our wants. We also learned the differences between good debt and bad debt. Not all debts are created equal! That is an important lesson. If a debt is going to make you money then seriously consider it. We learned that cash flow is what is remaining from our income after we pay all of our bills and expenses. We need to work on increasing our cash flow so that we can invest in the future and pay down our bad debts. Before we move on and KO! our bad debt, let us take a moment to pray and ask for God's guidance.

Dear Lord,

Thank You for dying for us. Thank You for reminding us that all things of this earth will come and go but You will remain forever. You are the risen Lord. Help us to keep our eyes on You. Please help us remain committed to managing our finances as responsible Christians. Lord, help us to want less and to be satisfied with simply knowing You. You are greater than any gift or possession we will ever come in contact with. As we continue to make sense of our finances please guide our footsteps so that we walk on the straight and narrow path with You.

In Jesus' name,

Amen

Chapter V
The KO Debt Plan

Now that we have compiled your personal financial statement (PFS), analyzed your income and expenses and looked at characteristics of each, it is time to take action. We are going to learn how to knock out (KO) our debts one at a time. It is these debts that hold us hostage and weigh the most on us. It is time to be free of these financial burdens. It will not be easy and there may be setbacks but we will continue to climb the hills because we know on the other side is great freedom in knowing we are no longer in bondage to our debtors. Remember, you are not in this alone. God is right by your side. If He is for us who can be against us?

Dear Lord,

We do not give You enough thanks. Please forgive us. We love You and wish to please You but we know we fall short. Lord, even for as well as we have tried to manage the gifts You have given us, we have come short. We have such a long way to go in order to fully comprehend Your love. Please remind us of Your presence as we start the hardest financial challenge of our lives. Help us to finish this marathon so that we can be prepared for the next. As we make daily decisions, however small or large, please guide us and remind us that each small decision is a part of the whole picture. Thank You for every day.

Amen

Stepping in the Ring

We want to KO our debt! That is, we want to knock out our bad debt. If you are in over your head with bad debt, imagine a month going by without having to make payments on any of these loans. Then imagine all of your loans paid off. Doesn't that feel good? Remember that feeling.

Does it pay to do a good deed?

That question is debatable but one thing is for sure, it worked for one man. He was on his way home when he noticed a broken-down limousine on the side of the road. The long black stretch limo had a flat tire. Out of the kindness of his heart, he pulled his truck to the side of the road and offered to change the tire so that the passengers and driver would not have to get their clothes dirty or endanger themselves on the busy highway. He was a living example of Christ; a servant. He fixed the flat and both cars went their separate ways. A few days later, he learned that the occupant of that limo, who he'd had the chance to meet while changing the flat, paid his mortgage in full. His good deed had been rewarded by the one and only Donald Trump. Wow! What a feeling to be mortgage free!

The Bible tells us to live all of life for Christ. It is not man who we are serving but the Lord Jesus Christ. (Colossians 3:23–24). It also tells us that whatever we do, let it be for God and not for a reward. Great is our reward in Heaven for being faithful servants.

Colossians 3:17 (NIV)

17 And whatever you do, whether in word or deed, do it all in the name of the Lord Jesus, giving thanks to God the Father through him.

We want to eliminate *all* of our bad debts, but we need to start with one at a time. Unfortunately, for most of us, the process will not be an overnight feat. It will be more like a long adventurous journey. The more debts you have the more time it may take. However, as you pay your first debt off you will gain momentum. With each bad debt you cast aside, you will pick up more and more drive and before long you will be cruising on Easy Street with the cruise control enabled.

Debts from Our PFS

Take a look at Expenses on your PFS. Write down all of the expenses that are loans or credit card balances below. You can choose to include or exclude your mortgage if you have one. The main thorn in our sides is our recurring bad debts that are not associated with an appreciating asset. That is, the debts that do not have an asset that is gaining value as time goes by. A car does not gain value. Your primary residence usually does, however, and this is why I will leave it up to you to include it or not on the list. If paying off your mortgage is part of your plan, then include it. That is the only exception that I would make. Include any home equity loans or lines of credit you may have in your KO plan. Fill in your bad debt below in Figure 2. Start with the debt that has the lowest balance and list it on the first line.

Key

- **Description:** Name of account.
- **Monthly Minimum Payment:** The minimum payment allowable. Most loans are a set payment but with credit cards your minimum payment may differ. We want the lowest you can pay without getting a penalty.* (Do not

- include a finance charge or interest as a "penalty" in this case. By penalty, I mean late fee, etc.)
- **Balance:** The amount that you currently owe on this account.

Figure 2- Bad Debt That We Are Going to KO!

Description	Monthy Minimum Payment	Balance
1.		
2.		
3.		
4.		
5.		

Bad Debt Example

Description	Monthy Minimum Payment	Balance
1. Credit Card	$85	$3,900
2. Car Loan #1	$263	$11,800
3. Personal Loan	$376	$12,500
4. Car Loan #2	$601	$16,800
5.		

Take a look at your list. Are the items listed in order from the lowest balance to the highest balance? That lowest one is going to be our first contender that gets KO'd!

KO – Featherweight (No. 1 on the list: lowest balance credit card)

We now have a list of our bad debts that we want to rid ourselves of. We are taking on the smallest of our debts first. That's a good thing because we are new to facing our debts. We are just starting out and do not want to overwhelm ourselves. We are not yet ready to get into the ring with Holyfield. Because we are starting small, we will win.

Look at your PFS and determine your current cash flow. Remember, you will need to subtract all of your expenses from your income. That will tell you how much money you have to work with to KO your debt. If you are Gold then apply your extra cash flow to your mortgage payment. For Silver, apply this extra cash flow to your lowest balance debt. This may be your mortgage as well.

Simplified Personal Financial Statement		Date:
Total Assets Value:	$167,500	
Total Liabilities Loan Balance:	$93,300	
NET WORTH:	$74,200	
Monthly Income:	$2,900	
Monthly Expenses:	**$2,500**	
Monthly **CASH FLOW:**	**$400**	

Bad Debt Example

Description	Monthly Minimum Payment	Balance
1. Credit Card	~~$85~~ $185	$3,900
2. Car Loan #1	$263	$11,800
3. Personal Loan	$376	$12,500
4. Car Loan #2	$601	$16,800
5.		

* Use $100 from your cash flow to pay extra on your lowest monthly debt.

If you do not have any cash flow then you will either have to continue making the minimum payments until the first debt is paid off or use one of our alternative methods for correcting your situation. For Bronze and Honorable Mention, we will get into mortgage refinance and consolidation loans shortly.

From our example, if our lowest bad debt balance is $3,900 and we have a $100 cash flow that we can use to pay towards it then add the $100 payment onto the minimum. Your total payment would be $185.

As you can see below, by adding $100 to your minimum payment you will accelerate the process of paying this bad debt off.

Normal payoff:

It will take you **69 months** to be rid of your debt. In that time, you will pay **$1,931.31 in interest**.

With extra $100 payment:

It will take you **25 months** to be rid of your debt. In that time, you will pay **$655.30 in interest**.

Once this bad debt has been paid off, we are ready for the next round. It is time to move up to the Welterweight and take on a stronger, bigger competitor. Fortunately, you are stronger, smarter and have more cash in hand now to KO No. 2 just as quickly as you did the Featherweight.

> **Important Note**
>
> You cannot KO your debt if you continue to make additional debt. This plan will only work if you do not make further bad debt purchases. You will need to stop spending. It is hard. Prayer is necessary. Pray before each purchase and ask God if you should make the purchase or wait.

KO – Welterweight - (No. 2 on the list: car loan #1)

We just KO'd our first bad debt from our list. Congratulations! We are no longer rookies. Following our example, we now have an extra $185 that we can apply toward our No. 2 bad debt, our car loan #1.

As we continue to make the minimum payments on the remainder of the items on our list, we will add the $185 to our regular payment for our car until it is paid off. Can you feel the momentum? Once this is paid off we will have a whopping $448 ($263 from the current car payment + $185 from our first KO payments) to add to our personal loan payments. We are paying our debts down with momentum. The more debts we pay off, the more money we have to put toward our remaining debts.

Old car payment: $263

New car payment: $263 + 185 = **$448**

KO – Middleweight (No. 3 on the list: personal loan)

By now you are seeing how this process works and your skills are being continually fine-tuned as you stave off bad debt and unnecessary wants and remain focused on living a financially stress-free life. You are probably feeling very good about your finances. You have turned your situation around. If you were on the border between Gold and Silver, or Silver and Bronze or Bronze and Honorable Mention, you probably took a step up on the podium.

Paying off a single debt is no easy feat so enjoy the moment. Do not revel in it. You are halfway there. As a result of paying off the credit card and the car loan #1, we now have $448 to apply to our personal loan that has been a thorn in our side for so long. Wow, instead of paying the requested $376 for our loan we are going to pay $824 now. We are saving interest and accelerating our payment schedule. A few jumbo payments like this and, now, we are more than halfway up the hill.

Old personal loan payment: $376
New personal loan payment: $376 + 448 = **$824**

KO – Heavyweight (No. 4 on the list: car loan #2)

By the time you get to the Heavyweight KO round, you have had your share of ups and downs. You have fallen but the good news is you have recovered. You are learning a habit that will guide you and your finances from this point forward. In order to get here you had to sacrifice. You probably prayed several times telling God that you can't do it or it's too hard or you just weren't meant to have money. Luckily, these negative thoughts did not take hold and you trusted and had faith in God to see you through.

When you accept Jesus as your savior, it does not mean life will always be peachy or perfect. You recognize that you cannot save yourself. It is through Christ that we are saved, by His grace alone; a gift we cannot earn. There will be ups and downs but we are not alone. You are not alone! Our caring Father is with us when we win the big victory and when we suffer a defeat.

The Heavyweight KO round is probably the easiest one you will experience. You know that you can beat debt and this is your last contender. You are going for the Gold and you are on your way. You have $824 that you can add to your payments on your last remaining car loan. You thought $601 was a large payment for a car. You are now going to pay $1,425. How fast do you think you can pay this off?

Old car loan #2 payment: $601

New car loan #2 payment: $601 + 824 = **$1,425**

DEBT FREE and Loving It!

Now what? How do you feel? What are you going to do with the $1,425 you do NOT have to pay to someone else this month? Are you ready for some more bad debt? It is tempting! It is very, very tempting! Beware: that is how the devil traps you every time. You think, "I have an extra $1,425 a month. A $600 monthly payment for a new car won't hurt that bad." Then, you get another car and then you buy some other junk and then you start using your credit cards again instead of using cash. Before you know it, you are right back where you started…or maybe even worse!

A New Beginning

Once your bad debts are paid off, you truly have a new beginning. You are wiser and will remain, hopefully, committed to managing your finances. You increased your cash flow considerably. Now, you can start looking for ways to invest your income. Do you still have a mortgage? You could start applying these funds toward it. When in doubt, do not spend it; put your extra cash in a savings account. When you want a new car try something new and pay cash for it! Do you remember the excitement of being a kid at Christmastime? At least for most of us, the anticipation was unbearable! We had to wait. We had no choice. Try that the next time you want to buy something. If you do not have the cash already saved, then save until you have enough for the item. Do not charge it. Make yourself wait. You will either appreciate the item that much more or you will decide you do not really need it. For me, it is kind of like not having call waiting on our telephone. It is a surprise every time I answer. A treat.

In the next few chapters, we are going to take a closer look at how to manage your income and invest for the future. We will look at some alternative options for Bronze and Honorable Mention, who were not quite ready to step into the ring in this chapter. You can always come back to this chapter to step into the ring with your debt; I highly recommend it. For most of you the lesson has been learned and there will be no need to revisit the KO Debt Plan.

Dear Lord,

You have been so good to us. You give us so many chances to "get it." Thank You for picking us up. Thank You for teaching us. Thank You for hills so that we can learn to climb. Thank You for hardship so that we can learn compassion. Thank You for defeat so that we can know victory. Thank You for our minds so that we can learn more about You. Thank You for Your love.

Amen

Chapter VI
Defining a Plan of Action

Now we are getting into the fun stuff. We are entering the meat and potatoes of this book. We have looked at our income and the KO plan for paying off our bad debt. Now we will look at a plan for daily living. This plan will serve as the foundation for your finances. If you stick within the limits or close to the limits of this plan, you will save yourself many unnecessary financial struggles. You will build up your asset column on your PFS and enjoy positive cash flow after all of your expenses have been paid.

Lord,

Thank You for bringing us to this moment. Open our minds so that we can see our finances in a different light. As we struggle to stay committed to the cause, please be with us and keep us focused. You say that all things are possible through You. You say with the faith of a mustard seed we can move mountains. Lord, give us the courage to move mountains and the faith to persevere.

In Jesus' name,

Amen

The 65/35 Plan

In a nutshell, the 65/35 plan is living on 65 percent of your income. Again, that is NET income that I am talking about. This means that when you add up all of your bad debt and expenses, they should not total more than 65 percent of all of your monthly NET income. If you were on the Gold podium, then you are already at this level. Good job! For Silver and below you will need to work on lowering your expenses using the KO plan in the last chapter. More help is on the way shortly.

Rule #1: Expenses Should Not Exceed 65% of NET Income.

With the remaining 35 percent, we are going to set aside 10 percent for tithing, 15 percent for our emergency/freedom fund and 10 percent for spending. So, if we take a $100 and break it down it will look like the following:

$100   Income

-$65   All expenses (65%)

-$10   Tithing (10%)

-$15   Emergency/Freedom Fund (15%)

-$10   Spending Cash (10%)

In the next chapter we will begin breaking these down in more detail. For now, let's get a grasp on where you are on a percentage basis.

Formula
Debt-to-Income Ratio (DTI) equals Expenses divided by Income

For example:

$1,500 expenses ÷ $2,000 income = 75% Debt-to-Income Ratio

What is your DTI ratio? Write it down:

Debt-to-Income Ratio: _____

The lower this number, the better. If your number is high then we will need to work on lowering it by using the KO plan or a few other methods that we will get to later. If you really think about it, doesn't $65 out of $100 seem high? It is the majority of our income. Do you see the freedom we would have by lowering our expenses? How does the 10 percent suggested tithing sit with you? Does it seem high? Ten dollars does not seem high but if you take 10 percent multiplied by the net income, it might seem a bit higher than you are comfortable with. How about the emergency/freedom fund? Do you currently have a cash reserve in case of an emergency? Wouldn't it be nice to have money in the bank just for emergencies? It would definitely offer some peace of mind. Finally, how about the spending cash? Does $10 seem too low? We work hard for our money; we should be able to spend more than 10 percent, right?

The 65/35 plan is designed so that budgeting is automatic. There is no need for envelopes to stash cash away for each bill. In the olden days that may have worked but in our modern age there would be way too many envelopes. Just the thought of trying to manage all of that gives me a headache.

My Great Grandma

My great-grandmother lived a long frugal life. She worked hard during her working years and saved more of her money than she spent. She and my great grandfather lived through two world wars, the Great Depression, the advent of television, several other wars and the births and deaths of many loved ones. She came from a time when businesses were closed on Sunday and there was no such thing as a 24/7/365 work schedule. She lived to be 102. She never experienced Internet banking, although it was around during the later years of her life. She talked "cents on the dollar." When I would talk to her, she would tell me how the bank was only giving her "two cents on the dollar... just two cents!" I always got a chuckle out of that, but her simplicity was something to learn from. She taught me how to budget my money. Her method included putting cash in envelopes for each of your bills. When the bill would come due, you would take out the cash and pay it. Then you would replenish the envelope. She did not have a mortgage or a car loan envelope. She believed in paying cash. If she did not have the cash then she would save until she could pay for it in full or just not buy it. She was a simple woman.

In our modern age, we have made everything complicated. We have more tools for managing and investing our money than all of the prior generations; however, we are ironically far more in debt.

We have bigger houses, fancier cars, nicer clothing, better schools, big screen TVs and all the modern conveniences that one could have only dreamed of in years past and we are still unsatisfied. Maybe if we got rid of some of the modern-day conveniences, more of our time would be spent on chores and less of our time would be spent spending our money.

Years ago, I heard a financial guru suggest the easiest way to save money was to get a part-time job. His suggestion was not simply one to yield us additional income, but also to keep us out of the stores. When we get bored or lonely, we often go on spending sprees. The part-time job would keep us from having the extra time to squander our money. I have seen this technique work for several people.

As much as I loved my great-grandmother, I am not a fan of the envelope system. Actually, I am not a fan of budgeting—period. It is too much like work and finances should be fun. What are you most likely to stick with, something that feels like work or something that you actually enjoy doing? When you break down your bills individually, it becomes too complicated and too much to manage. That is why I stick with a percentage-based system; a general system that is easy to follow, is more automatic and less like work. We can break down each element of the system if necessary.

To get a good grasp of the 65/35 plan, let us look at an example. Notice Joe's PFS below. Joe has a net income of $2,000 per month. His monthly bills total $1,300. If we use the formula (Expenses ÷ Income) x 100 for calculating his DTI ratio he is at 65 percent.

Simplified Personal Financial Statement	Date:
Total Assets Value:	$150,000
Total Liabilities Loan Balance:	$120,000
Total Assets Value:	$30,000
Monthly Income:	$2,000
Monthly Expenses:	$1,300
Monthy CASH FLOW:	**$700 (65% Expense)**

Joe's DTI ratio: ($1,300 ÷ $2,000) x 100 = 65%

Joe's debt is within a good range. He has 35 percent of his net income remaining after expenses with which to build an emergency fund, tithe and spend how he pleases.

The 65/35 Breakdown

- **65% Max Total Expenses**
- **10% Tithing**
- **15% Emergency/Freedom Fund**
- **10% Spending Cash**

This plan allows for some flexibility. If we remember and follow Rule No. 1 (expenses max. = 65 percent of NET income), then our finances should rarely get out of hand. We will look into ways to safeguard yourself when unforeseen expenses do come your way. Usually, these miscellaneous expenses seem to negatively affect our finances the most. As we break down the plan, remember that no matter how you choose to get a grip on your finances it takes discipline. God knows we are not perfect. We make mistakes. As we learn and strive to improve upon our current situation, we need to try really hard to minimize the mistakes we make. That is, we need to recognize our behavior so that our financial slip-ups become smaller and smaller. Eventually, as responsible managers we will have the power to distinguish and overcome our temptations.

Before I made a commitment to manage my finances more responsibly, I did not do too badly. For the most part, I was living a fairly stress-free financial life. My spending was in check, my assets were increasing and my liabilities (debts) were within a reasonable range. But, all of a sudden it would hit me. I would make the big purchase. It would be a car or a large recording studio piece of equipment. My positive cash flow would be practically gone. Then I would be good for a while and pay off my debt. A few months would go by and bam! I would do the same thing over again. It was a constant vicious cycle. Good then bad, then good again, and then bad again. I said this *was* the way it was before I made a commitment. If we are going to do anything in life, we should do it with all of our hearts. When you make a commitment to improve your finances you are telling the world that you will sacrifice if necessary, you will not be jealous of what your neighbors or friends have, you are not in competition with the Joneses, you will live for the Lord and you will pray often for guidance.

Dear Lord,

You are Creator of all. You have gifted us with so many beautiful things. Help us to recognize all, both physically and spiritually, that we have been entrusted with. Lord, continue to bless us and expand our territory. Remind us that with more blessings come more responsibilities. Fill us with Your Spirit. We confess that we have sinned against You and we ask for Your forgiveness. As move forward with our financial journeys, Lord, please help us to stay focused on and committed to improving our current situations. Thank you for today and tomorrow.

Amen

Chapter VII
Living on 65% of Your Income

Some people may argue that 65 percent of NET income is simply not enough to live on. I agree. That is *if* your real intentions are on impressing others and indulging yourself in all of life's little luxuries. It may be impossible if your lone desire is to please only yourself while you are alive. Unfortunately, many people in modern society think that they should be "first." Savvy marketing companies have come up with slogans to brainwash you into this callous way of thinking, with catch phrases such as "It's all about you," and "Because I'm worth it." The truth is that we need to put others first. We also need to be content with what we have. If we are not content with what we have today, we will not be satisfied with what we get tomorrow. My point is that if we start putting others' needs before our own, then we will be more likely to find true happiness and contentment. Conversely, we will be less likely to try to find happiness in material possessions and status symbols.

Dear Lord,

We give You thanks for all of life's necessities. We thank You for food on our tables, clothing on our bodies and shelter to protect our families. We thank You for revealing Your love to us and for giving us the Word to live our lives by. We thank You for the opportunity to serve. Lord, please keep us focused on helping and loving Your children. Allow us to enjoy life's finer things without becoming fixated on them, remembering always to keep You first in our hearts. As we continue to learn about our finances, Lord, please guide us and comfort us when we feel low. Remind us of the hope we can have in Jesus Christ.

Amen

A Contrary Opinion – Getting a Mortgage

Since our housing expense is most likely the largest expense we will carry every month, we are going to take a closer look at mortgages. If you are renting, the same can be applied to your rental payments as well. Depending on whom you talk with, most people will offer differing opinions on what percentage you should be comfortable having as your DTI ratio. Most real estate agents and mortgage brokers may argue that 65 percent is too low. When they determine how much of a housing payment you can handle, they use your *gross* pay. Gross pay is your income before taxes and deductions. The maximum amount of money that a mortgage lender will allow you to borrow usually depends on two things:

1. **Maximum Mortgage Payment (MMP)**

    The MMP cannot exceed 28 percent of your annual gross (pre-tax) income. This is the most your mortgage payment can be when you include the monthly principal, interest, estimated taxes and homeowners insurance.

To calculate the MMP, multiply your annual salary by 0.28, then divide by 12 (months). The answer is your maximum housing expense.

Maximum housing expense (MMP) = annual salary x 0.28 ÷ 12 (months)

2. Maximum Monthly Debt (MMD)

The MMD should not exceed 36 percent of your gross (pre-tax) income. It is the total "back-end" debt that you are obligated to pay, such as credit cards, car loans, student loans, other mortgages, child support/alimony and condominium fees. This does not include any utilities, groceries, life insurance or other monthly bills that you may have. To calculate your MMD, multiply your annual salary by 0.36, then divide by 12 (months). The answer is your maximum allowable DTI ratio.

Maximum allowable debt-to-income ratio (MMD) = annual salary x 0.36 ÷ 12 (months)

Depending on what loan product you choose the percentages will vary. The best way to get a mortgage if you need to borrow for a house (and who doesn't?) is to save and get a conventional loan. You will save thousands of dollars in fees in interest over the life of the loan. Below are typical percentages for both conventional and FHA loans. An FHA (Federal Housing Administration) loan is a first-time homebuyer's product.

Loan Types

- **Conventional loans:**

  Housing costs: 26–28 percent of monthly gross income.

  Housing plus debt costs: 33–36 percent of monthly gross income.

  Required down payment: typically 20 percent of the purchase price.

- **FHA loans:**

  Housing costs: 29 percent of monthly gross income.

  Housing plus debt costs: 41 percent of monthly gross income.

  Required down payment: typically 5 percent of purchase price.

Example of MMP and MMD

Say you make $20,000 a year. Banks would tell you that you could afford a maximum housing payment of $467. (Your annual gross (pre-tax) salary ($20,000) multiplied by 28% (.28) equals $5,600. Divided by 12 (months) equals $466.66.)

In addition, your maximum monthly debt could not exceed 36%, which comes to $600. (Your annual gross (pre-tax) salary multiplied by 36% (.36) equals $7,200. Divided by 12 (months) equals $600.)

While I agree that these ratios help people from overextending themselves, I also believe that they may still be a bit too generous. My reasoning is this.

Why do I think banks' MMP and MMD percentages are too high?

1. First off, they are using your annual gross (PRE-TAX) income. Unless you get paid monthly, it would be better for you to use four weeks of income instead. If you are paid biweekly you end up with two extra pays a year. If you get paid weekly you have five months

142

with five paychecks and seven months with four paychecks. So, basically, unless you are getting paid a lump sum each month you are better off taking two biweekly pays or four weekly pays as your monthly total. The majority of the months only have four weeks so that's what you will have to work with the majority of the time unless you are really good with saving and know how to budget your money well.

How does this look based on your pay schedule?

Let's use $52,000 as a salary example to make the math easy.

Salary: $52,000

Weekly: $1,000 x 4 = $4,000 (for 7 months) and $5,000 (for 5 months)

Biweekly: $2,000 x 2 = $4,000 (for 10 months) and $6,000 (for 2 months)

Monthly: $4,333 (for 12 months)

As you will notice for most months there will only be $4,000 to work with to pay all of your bills. We should consider the months when you get the extra pay as a bonus.

We typically think from the top. We like to think that our salaries are higher than they really are. If we have a few months at $5,000, we start thinking that is the norm but in reality it is not. It is almost $700 too much on average and $1,000 too much the majority of the time.

2. Secondly, they are still talking in terms of gross (PRE-TAX) income. Nobody gets to keep 100 percent of his pay. We need to look at spending our dollars in terms of NET income. That is the only money we can use for writing checks and paying our bills. Lenders have us thinking in terms of gross when we really need to be basing everything on our NET (after-tax/deductions) income.

The Bank's Formula Applied to Real Life

Let's say you make $1,667 a month in gross wages. (Annual gross salary of $20,000 divided by 12 (months).) The banks allow you 28 percent, which means the bank feels confident that you can afford a payment of $467 per month for principal, interest, taxes and insurance. With all of your other debts and obligations, you can use up to 36 percent of your gross income for a maximum of $600.

Gross Income: $1,667

Maximum Monthly Debt: $600 (36% of $1,667)

In this scenario, you will get a mortgage of about $55,000 at a 7 percent interest rate amortized over 30 years and your monthly payments will be around $467. Keep in mind that the 36 percent does not include other expenses associated with owning a home, such as maintenance, utility bills and so on and so forth.

MMD Breakdown

Mortgage: $55,000

Principal/Interest: $367 month

Taxes/Insurance: $100 month

Other Loan Debt Max: $133 month

Total: $600 Maximum Monthly Debt

The mortgage principal and interest would be around $367, and the taxes and insurance would add an extra $100. That gives us a total of $467 for our mortgage, taxes, insurance, yet still does not include our utilities and other housing-related expenses. The remaining $133 is the maximum additional loan/obligations you can have in addition to your housing expense. This could be for a car loan or student loan or some other debt.

A Closer Look

Now let's take a closer look at this. To start, this is 36 percent of our *gross* income. On average, the NET income would be $1,155 after taxes and deductions. If we take this same $600 and compare it with our net (after-tax/deductions) income, we are looking at 48 percent of our income! We are already at 48 percent and we have not turned on the heat, water/sewer, telephone, bought groceries or even considered having to buy gas for our car. Remember, these are the basic living expenses. We have not even touched on the miscellaneous expenses that often ruin a budget.

Debt Ratio Based on NET Income

$1,155	NET income
-600	Maximum monthly debt
-160	Utilities (Heat/water/sewer/gas/telephone)
- 80	Automobile gasoline ($20 per week)
-160	Groceries ($40 per week)
$155	**TOTAL**

Even with using conservative numbers above, we are looking at normal living expenses of 80 percent of our NET income. Can you see how money might get tight if you are stretching your debt-to-income like this? In addition, if we use the NET income amount for the majority of months, this number increases even further.

Salary Breakdown

Salary: $20,000

Weekly:

$385 x 4 = $1,540 (for 7 months) and $1,925 (for 5 months)

Biweekly:

$770 x 2 = $1,540 (for 10 months) and

$2,310 (for 2 months)

Monthly:

$1,667 (for 12 months)

If we use $1,540 as our gross (pre-tax) income, our net pay would end up being around $1,155 (Gross ($1,540) minus 25 percent (average tax/deductions)). That makes our $1,000-a-month living expenses a whopping 87 percent of our net income. Do you see where I am going with this?

Understand that just because a real estate agent or a banker tells you that you can afford "x amount of dollars" for a mortgage does not mean that they have your best interest at heart. You need to do and understand the math for yourself. Use your own rules. Use your NET income and only use four weeks of it. You may find it limiting at first but eventually you will reap the benefits.

Benefits of Using Your NET Income When Getting a Mortgage

- Unexpected expenses will not break your budget.
- Your bank accounts will go up instead of staying flat or going down.
- You will keep your expenses within your 65 percent goal.
- Your housing expense will be within a comfortable range.

Keep in mind that my observations have been based solely on obtaining a conventional mortgage with a 20 percent down payment and closing costs paid at the time of settlement. FHA and VA loans offer even higher debt-to-income ratios. These programs were designed to assist first-time homebuyers in purchasing a house with little money down. Again, I am not advising against these programs. I am suggesting that you look at what your true monthly income is and what percentages you want to base your monthly payments on.

You can apply these same percentages to the price you are paying for rent as well. Housing will most likely be the largest bill you pay each month so you need to be sure it fits within your budget.

Overextending Your Mortgage

When you meet with mortgage brokers, you can quickly become overwhelmed by all of the products that are available today. They have zero down mortgages, interest only mortgages, conventional (which are probably not as common as some of the other products now) and a bunch of other options. Without going into the details of all the loans that are available today, I will highlight a few that should be avoided and why.

Zero Down Loans

As you probably have guessed, a zero down loan requires no money to close the deal. When you do not bring anything to the table, you are at more of a risk for the lender so your rates and fees are going to be higher. Since the loan is for more than 80 percent of the property value, you will be forced to pay Private Mortgage Insurance (PMI).

PMI protects your lender in the event you default on your loan. You pay for it and they get the protection. You can expect to pay on average around $1,500 a year for PMI on a $200,000 loan. Another issue with a zero down loan is the assumptions you make. You are assuming your property will increase in value and not go down. Property values usually go up in value but they can come down. Many overpriced areas take huge hits when the market corrects itself and people end up with a mortgage for twice the value of the house. In those cases, you are stuck in your house until you pay it down or you can sell it for a loss. Many have just walked away in foreclosure.

TIP: Save and put 20 percent down when you buy a house. You qualify for a conventional loan, get better rates and will not have to pay PMI.

The 80/20 Loan

Much like a zero down loan, you do not need any down payment money for an 80/20. This was the lender's slick way of giving you one hundred percent of the purchase price (and maybe closing costs), without having to get PMI. Again, you are bringing nothing to the table so your fees and rates will probably be higher since you are considered a high-risk customer. You have some of the same issues with the 80/20 as you do with zero down loans. When you use this product you start with no equity in your new house. You also assume it will increase in value. On top of that, you have two loans to pay. The first is usually a conventional loan and the second is usually in the form of a home equity loan. Two payments equals two bills. We want to eliminate bills not add two more to our list.

Interest Only (IO) Loan

As housing prices have soared in the last few years, the interest only loan business has taken off. Again, people are counting on their property values to increase. The argument is that as time goes by the property will increase in value and as it increases, your equity in the house will increase while your mortgage (what you owe on it) stays the same. "Interest"-ing idea! Pun intended.

You hear both pros and cons regarding this type of mortgage. There are a few misconceptions that you should be aware of. The first misconception is that your interest rate is fixed. Most of the time, IO loans are adjustable rate loans. The second is that the interest rates are better than conventional loans. This is a huge misconception and untrue. The third reason not to get an IO loan is you may be forced to pay PMI. Remember, PMI is paying for something that protects the lender, not you. You are giving that money away every month. The last point I want to make about IO loans is that these are not 30-year loans. Most of them are amortized and due in seven, 10 or 15 years. At that time, you will need to refinance or pay the balance in full. Unless you have paid extra while making your IO payments, you will still owe exactly the same as when you got the mortgage. I hope that if you chose this route, your property value went up, otherwise you may be stuck or out of a house.

Results of Overextending

Unfortunately, in our society most people do not want to save for the 20 percent down payment. They also do not want to wait. These alternative loan products offer you the get-it-now-and-pay-later option. The problem is that these are risky products for the common person. If you do not have the 20 percent to put down on the house, then you probably do not have the discipline to use these types of loans. As more and more people choose these products we will see more and more bankruptcies and foreclosures.

When we get in these situations where we think we need more than we are capable of handling financially, we need to pray for focus. Are we putting more importance on earthly things? How will our budget be affected? We will still be in our 65 percent debt-to-income ratio? How about our net worth?

The bottom line is if you cannot go the conventional loan route then you probably should wait until you can. Waiting is hard. It takes discipline. Lenders and real estate agents may argue against it. The thing to remember is that you are the one who will be stuck with the bill and the lifestyle as a result. When buying a house, save 20 percent or more for a down payment and use conservative numbers when determining what you can afford. It may be a smaller house than you think you deserve or want but that is OK. You can always sell and buy a bigger house after you have saved more money and your income has increased. Your housing payment will probably be your biggest expense, so take extra special care before making a decision.

Retirement

At this point, we have looked at our expenses, income, assets and liabilities. We have looked our debt-to-income ratios and how a mortgage should fit into the big picture of our finances. Before we get into what should make up the remainder of the first 65 percent of your income, I want to take another look at retirement.

We briefly touched on retirement earlier. If you recall, we used the following formula.

Retirement = Passive Income Greater Than Monthly Expenses

Retirement is possible when our passive income from businesses, real estate, dividends, stocks and bonds exceeds our monthly expenses. We also talked briefly about investing in businesses and real estate. I said before that these two areas might not be comfortable for your personality. While I am all for you expanding your territory and moving out of your comfort zone, I want to offer the potentially safest and easiest way for you to prepare for a successful retirement.

The 401(k) Retirement Plan

It is easy to see that most people are living for today. They are not thinking of the long-term consequences of their actions or inactions. You have probably seen the commercial where a person shows all of his material possessions and status symbols—big house, new car, big lawn mower and country club membership—and then declares: "How do I do it? I am up to my eyeballs in debt!"

Do you know why this commercial is so funny? It is because it is so true! This is most of America. We have chosen the have-it-now-and-pay-for-it-later mentality. As a result, many are forgoing the idea of "paying yourself" first. A new philosophy people are using today is making their house their retirement plan. My questions to them are: "Where are you going to live? And how are you going to pay your living expenses?" A house is great and usually a nice asset to have but we need to put our coins in different baskets.

Pay Yourself First

The easiest way to build a retirement portfolio is by participating in your company's 401(k) retirement plan. By contributing to a 401(k) plan, you are paying yourself first. That is, BEFORE you pay the government. The money you put in comes right off the top of your check, before taxes. As a result, you have more of your money invested. In addition, when you invest in your 401(k) you enjoy tax breaks. By taking the investment right off the top, your taxable income is lowered. For example, if you make $60,000 gross income and contribute 10 percent (of that gross income), you are only responsible for paying taxes on $54,000. You have paid yourself $6,000 that will grow tax-free.

Employer Match

Many businesses match employee contributions, either fully or partially. Although they are not legally obligated to match contributions, it's widely practiced and a very common benefit. Most employers will match fifty cents on the dollar, up to 6 percent of your salary. Therefore, at the very least you should contribute 6 percent a year so that you take full advantage of this employer match. If you cannot max out the 401(k) benefit, you should at least try to reach the limit that your employer will match. This is free money for you once you are one hundred percent vested in the plan. Usually it takes five years to become fully invested with a company. Check with your company for more information on vesting.

Example of Employer Match

- 401(k) (pre-tax) contribution: $1,800 (6% of $30,000 gross income)
- Matching company contribution: $900 (50 cents up to 6% of gross income)

Start Now!

Many people think they cannot afford to have part of their paycheck missing every week. I have had several people tell me that they just do not have the extra money to invest. The problem is they will have even less when they are ready to retire. The one thing you cannot buy is time, and time works wonders when it comes to our retirement. The sooner you start investing the better. For each dollar you invest, you are practically doubling your money when you count the employer contribution and the tax savings. The dollar that you invest is really only, maybe, 75 cents after taxes and deductions, so you will not see that big of a difference in your net (post-tax/deductions) take-home pay. On the other hand, over time you will see considerable growth when you stick with the plan.

Why You Should Invest 10% of Your Income

The most important part of preparing for retirement, regardless if it is 10 or 30 years down the road, is getting started. Don't let the subject intimidate you.

A lot of people feel like they are clueless when it comes to investing, and because it is new territory for them they put it off. With 401(k)s there are limitations on what you can invest your money in and, as a result, you are less likely to fail. Overall, these plans average 9 percent over the long haul. The more you contribute, the more you have to gain. The minimum I would suggest investing is 6 percent. This number is usually the magic number that employers will match. You can invest up to 25 percent (with a ceiling of $15,000) of your annual gross income if you are under 50 years old, and up to $18,000 if you are over 50 as of this writing.

I personally like 10 percent because it is right in the middle of the road. The extra 4 percent really helps but it does not feel like a big hit to your paycheck. One year I maxed out my contributions because my finances permitted it. Ultimately it comes down to what you feel comfortable contributing. The idea is to start now. The chart below shows the differences between investing 2 percent and 10 percent of a $50,000 gross annual salary over a 10-, 20- and 30-year span, assuming an average rate of return of 8 percent.

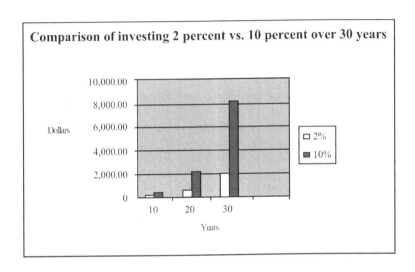

Comparison of investing 2 percent vs. 10 percent over 30 years

What Do I Invest In?

One of the great things about technology is the Internet. We have access to everything whenever we want it. (Note: This could be a bad thing if we do not take the time to breathe, slow down and think about our purchases.) I would go as far as to say that probably everyone's retirement plans are now on the Web and can be accessed by the enrollee.

Years ago, you had to wait for your statement to arrive in the mail, or contact the plan administrator if you had any questions. Now you have instant access. With all this access, the managers of these 401(k) plans have been pretty good about explaining what they offer. Many offer suggestions on what to invest in based on your current situation. Typically, the rule of thumb is as follows:

- **Young** – you have time on your hands, invest in high risk plan.
- **Mid-career** – start transferring to a moderate investment package.
- **Closer to retirement** – move to a more conservative plan.

401(k) No-No's

Regardless of where you are in your life, there are a few things you should try to avoid. The first is cashing out your retirement early. Not only will you get taxed on the funds at your current tax rate but you will also pay large penalties. All that free money that you received from your employer, as well as the tax-free gains, will be gone and you will be throwing all of the time that you used out the window. You can expect to lose 40 percent of the balance that you cash out.

Another tempting proposition to avoid is borrowing from your 401(k). This should also be a last resort in times of crisis. When you borrow from your 401(k), you are on the hook to pay yourself back at a decent interest rate. It sounds good that you are paying yourself interest but you are losing all of the compounding factors of your investments. The larger amount you have compounding the larger return you will get. Likewise for the opposite, if you have a small amount compounding you will experience a smaller return. If you decide to leave your company, you will either need to pay in full the loan amount or be on the hook for the same cash-out penalties described in the previous paragraph. The bottom line is if you really need the money, get a personal or home equity loan first.

In conclusion, before we even get to living on 65 percent of our net income, we need to make sure we take care of investing in our future.

The Remainder of Your First 65%

Before you even get to the net portion (after-tax/deductions) of your paycheck you should invest in your retirement plan. Then with the first 65 percent (net), allocate a large portion of your pay toward your housing expense, which will be either your mortgage or your rent. The remainder should be used for your essential living expenses. When I say "essential," I mean your "needs" not "wants." (Refer to Chapter IV for a refresher.) If your loans are pushing you over the 65 percent limit, then use the KO plan to knock them out. We will look into some other options for paying down your loan debt shortly. In the meantime, let's review what we have so far.

Pre-tax
- Income (GROSS) → invest 10% in 401(k)

Post-tax – 65%
- Paycheck (NET)

  → Mortgage (including taxes, insurance, home association fees, etc.)

  → Essential Living Expenses

  → Electric

  → Water/Sewer

  → Food (not dining out)

→ Heat

→ Telephone (not cell phones)

→ Health

→ Fuel (auto gas)

→ Loans

    → Personal

    → Home Equity

    → Credit Cards

    → School Loans

Essential Living Expenses

Defining what is essential and non-essential is crucial to your success. We need to look at our expenses on a daily basis. Each time we consider making a purchase, we need to think about how this will affect our plan. We need to ask ourselves, "Is this purchase justified? Is this a want or a need?" before we use the first 65 percent of net income to buy it.

As a business, the best way to secure your future is to get return customers. The best customers for a business are the ones who are locked in to paying each and every month. These are the "recurring customer." Great for business but can be very bad for you and your budget.

Cell Phone Scenario

When you sign up for a new cell phone, they have you for most likely two years. You sign a contract to pay them for this agreed-upon length of time. Let's take a look at the big picture when purchasing a cell phone. You go and buy a cell phone. No, actually, let's assume they give you the phone for free. You are only responsible for the monthly fees. If we assume you take the average cell phone package, you are looking at $39.95 a month. With a contract of two years, you can expect to pay a total of $958.80 before taxes. By getting a free phone and signing the agreement, you just made a $1,000 purchase.

Conclusion

The point here is not to make you feel guilty about having some of life's luxuries. It is about being aware of each and every purchase you make and how it may impact your finances. God has blessed us with many treats and bonuses. My suggestion is that we remember that these are just that. If we are disciplined and stay true to how God would have us live our financial lives, we will find beauty and pleasure in many things that do not cost a dime. We will enjoy the beauty of the outdoors by going for a walk or hike with our family. We will enjoy using our imaginations while reading a great book. We will spend some time studying the Bible and learning more about our wonderful maker. We will slow down and see, not just look, but actually experience our spouse and children, and marvel at their loveliness. We will also find that our financial lives bring happiness to us.

Not by looking at what we have accumulated, but by being content knowing that we are living within our means. By having confidence that we are ready should an emergency arise, and by having the pleasure to give back to God as he has so graciously given to us. Have you heard the phrase, "The best things in life are free"? Maybe there is some truth to that!

Dear Lord,

Thank You for this beautiful day. Thank You for the breath of life you breathe into us. Please be with us as we touch up or completely repaint our financial pictures. Remind us of our beautiful surroundings that you have made for us to enjoy for free. Be with us as we struggle with contentment in a society that offers false hope in material possessions. We know that the excitement is short-lived in these things. Lord, help us to stay focused on You, who are the only source of true contentment.

In Jesus' name,
Amen

Chapter VIII

Investing 10% in Your Spiritual Well Being

Money and religion are two very touchy subjects when it comes to conversation. Most people would rather avoid the topics. When you mix the two and talk about tithing, you get even tighter lips. Opinions vary on how much you should give and where you should give. Many will offer their time as a means of giving, in order to avoid the departure of their money. It has long been a touchy subject and I would like to offer a new light on the topic. Before we begin let us pray.

Dear Lord,

You are God! Sometimes we need reminded of this simple fact. All things come from You and all things will return to You. Thank You for Your gifts! Please accept our time and offerings as gifts of our gratefulness to You. Give us the faith to give without apprehension. Open our hearts and minds to hear new ideas and meditate on them. Open our eyes so that we may see You and not be distracted. We love You, Lord. Help us to be Your humble servants.

Amen

Tithe

I recently talked with a friend about tithing and he asked me, "What exactly is a tithe?" I was surprised that he had never heard of the term. I knew what it meant to me but not the dictionary definition.

The word "tithe" actually means one-tenth. It is a tenth of one's annual income contributed voluntarily or as a levy (tax) for the support of clergy and/or a church. A tenth, in other words—10 percent! That seems high doesn't it? I have had a few people ask me what I thought was the proper amount to give. In a nutshell, I like the idea of giving twice of the amount that you are comfortable with until you reach at least 10 percent. (Remember the guy from the beginning of the book? I liked his approach—give 'til it hurts.)

For example, if my comfort level is giving $25 a week, but 10 percent of my income is really $75, I force myself to give $50 ($25 x 2). As I become more and more comfortable, I will then double it again. It won't be long before 10 percent does not seem so bad. Before we look at the amount we should give let us look at *why* we should give.

Why Should We Give?

I. As an Act of Faith

When we give back to God, we are displaying an act of faith. We are displaying to God that we trust in Him and that we acknowledge that all things come from Him. By giving back, we place our faith in God that He will provide for us. He is the maker of all things and we are just the managers. We give as recognition that this is God's Earth.

---

1 Corinthians 8:6

yet for us there is but one God, the Father, from whom all things came and for whom we live; and there is but one Lord, Jesus Christ, through whom all things came and through whom we live.

Psalm 24:1

The earth is the Lord's and everything in it, the world, and all who live in it

---

II. To Help Those in Need

This past December I went Christmas caroling with our church. We sang and delivered bags of gifts to quite a few families that were having financially hard times.

Before we departed the church, we prayed and were prepped with a few words. We were told not to judge the recipients of these gifts. We were also told that we may not agree with their lifestyles but, again, we should not be judgmental.

While I found it easy to not judge, I found it difficult to not judge the lifestyles they had chosen. It really got me thinking. The more I thought about it the more convicted I became. Deep down I harshly judged those people for choosing the wrong path and choices. But the truth came to me and hit me like a ton of bricks. I am just as guilty! If we compared my lifestyle of spending to theirs, you would see that I have made some unnecessary foolish purchases myself! It reminded me of the following verse.

> **John 8:7**
>
> *So when they continued asking him, he lifted up himself, and said unto them, He that is without sin among you, let him first cast a stone at her.*

Scripture calls us to help the poor and needy. In the following passage, the people of Israel were called to donate the third year of crops for those in need—the Levites (who had no allotment or inheritance of their own).

> **Deuteronomy 14:28–29 (KJV)**
>
> *28 At the end of three years thou shalt bring forth all the tithe of thine increase the same year, and shalt lay it up within thy gates:*
> *29And the Levite, (because he hath no part nor inheritance with thee,) and the stranger, and the fatherless, and the widow, which are within thy gates, shall come, and shall eat and be satisfied; that the LORD thy God may bless thee in all the work of thine hand which thou doest.*

III. For the Life of the Church

No matter where you work, at some time or another you will be asked to donate to an event or a charitable cause. A lot of these opportunities are good and bring favorable returns for the good of man. Unfortunately, they do not support the church.

I am not going to tell you to stop contributing to these, but I will suggest that you do not sacrifice your tithe to the church as a result. We need to make our first priority as Christians to further the kingdom of God by supporting our local churches. While some may argue that giving is the main point, I would argue that targeted giving is what we should strive for. Just like when we make purchases, we also need to look at where our money goes and how it is used when we tithe.

IV. As a Sacrifice

Jesus Christ sacrificed one hundred percent of his being so that we may live. If we had to save ourselves, we would all fail. He died so that we may live. He loves us and offered himself as the ultimate sacrifice. What can we do to show our love for him? We can start by praying. Next we can study and learn all we can about this magnificent God in the Bible. The next thing we can do is begin tithing. Giving money away is not easy. It is hard for us to part with our money especially when we are not getting something of a material nature in return. The same goes for spiritual gifts. We cannot expect to get a spiritual blessing from our tithe either. When we tithe, we need to do it as a form of appreciation, thankfulness, faithfulness and love for our Father in heaven.

How Much Should We Give?

As I mentioned before there are many opinions on how much you should tithe. The Bible uses the example in Israel in which 1/10 (tithe) was to be used for the poor and needy. Again, tithe literally means a tenth. Many church officials use 10 percent of your gross income as the target. Still others feel that their service is their tithe. I believe that God is calling us on a personal level to Him when it comes to tithing. He is saying "come" with His arms wide open. Yet many are afraid to take that step. We see Him at the other side of a ravine and we are afraid to take the leap of faith toward Him. We, like Peter, are walking on water and then doubt and start to sink. We are of little faith. God is right in front of us as a proud father, longing for us to put our total trust in Him. By making the sacrifice and tithing our money, we are declaring our faith and hope in Him.

Strive to Tithe

Based on scripture, I believe we should strive to tithe 10 percent of our paycheck—our net pay, which is after taxes and deductions.

If you take home $500, you should set $50 as your target for tithing. If you bring home $1,000 then you should set $100 as your target. I say target because depending on our current financial situations—for example if you were Bronze or Honorable Mention on the podium—you may have to give less to start. Like controlling our spending it is also difficult to be persistent with our giving. We need to make it a habit. Like Christ sacrificed Himself for us, maybe we need to sacrifice a couple of things for Him. Try eating at home when we get the urge to order take-out. Try reading a book when we feel like going out to the movies. (Maybe that book could be the Bible.) Maybe we could wait one more month for those fancy sneakers that we really "need" and instead give the money that we saved to our church. Maybe we can sacrifice for Christ. There is really no "maybe" about it; we need to make these sacrifices.

Words of Caution

Concluding I wanted to offer some words of caution with regards to tithing. As we are inspired to give, we should be responsible with our giving as well.

God does not want us to donate all of our paycheck to the church and forget about paying our bills at home. We are to be responsible servants and pay the money that is due to our lenders. Our challenge is to pay our bills down and to become better managers of our finances so that we can give more.

Another word of caution is about motivational speakers. Some will tell you to give and to give freely. They will tell you that for each dollar you give you will get two dollars in return. They will tell you that for each person you help, two people will in turn help you. They try to affirm this by using the law of reciprocity. The basic concept is "I'll scratch your back if you scratch mine." The key flaw in this idea is the expectation. You are giving with the hope, or most likely, with the expectation that you will receive a two-fold return. Another flaw with the whole idea is the haphazard focus of where to give. Like investing our money for retirement, we need to invest our gifts just as wisely for the betterment of man and society.

When we give, we need to give from our heart and expect *nothing* in return. By grace alone are we saved. We cannot earn our own ticket to heaven. It is graciously given to us by believing in Jesus Christ. We need to have faith and trust in the Lord alone and not expect a dime in return. God owes us nothing but as a generous Father, He will provide.

Dear Lord,

When we sit back and look at all of the blessings You have bestowed upon us in our lives, it leaves us in awe. We are not worthy of any of these gifts, yet as a loving Father you continually provide for us. We love You Lord and thank You. You are God, maker of all things. Accept our gifts as a sacrifice to be used to further Your kingdom. Give us the courage to have faith that You will provide for us and our families. Lord, we love You and thank You for all things.

Amen

Chapter IX

Saving 15%–The Emergency/Freedom Fund

At this point in the game, we are still working on ways of financially securing our future. We have examined ways to knock out our debt, learned a little about investing and looked at the importance of tithing. In this chapter, we will look at our next 15 percent of net income. We will learn how to safeguard ourselves from unexpected expenses and fall back on an age-old principal of only buying when you have the cash. Before we begin let us be reminded that all plans take commitment to be successful. Let us ask the Lord to keep us steadfast in this commitment to serve Him and manage our finances.

Dear Lord,

Thank You for Your commitment to us! So often we roam around like lost sheep, from one thing to the next, only to find that we are never satisfied. We think we will find peace in this and in that and eventually discover that this pleasure is forever fleeting. Lord, forgive us for these failures. Let us stay focused only on You; the real source of peace. Keep us committed to You and to changing our lifestyles for the better. Strengthen us as we are tempted and keep us on the narrow road. Lord, You are the giver and creator of all. Help us to remember to trust in You always.

In Jesus' name,
Amen

The Emergency Fund

As you probably have guessed by its name, the emergency fund is simply for that—emergencies. This money is to be put away and never touched unless absolutely necessary.

Your family vacation is not considered an emergency. Although I believe that vacations are crucial for a healthy family and work-life balance, financing them should not come from your emergency fund. We will talk about where the costs of vacations and other fun things should come from later. First, let us define an emergency.

What Is an Emergency?

An emergency is the loss of your job, major medical bills, a disabling injury, or a costly auto or house repair to name a few. These are the nuts and bolts of what you should access your emergency fund in order to pay. If you have the cash to pay for the auto or home repair then use it. The idea is to only use the emergency fund when absolutely necessary. While some may disagree, I believe that using a line of credit or credit card is not the best way to handle a financial crisis. We want to avoid methods that will end up costing us in the long run.

One man argues that he will "borrow against his retirement if an emergency comes up." A woman states, "I don't feel comfortable having that money just sitting idle." These are both interesting statements.

Borrowing Against Your Retirement

First, for this to even be a possibility you need to have a decent amount of money in your retirement to begin with. According to MetLife (MMI00027 (0805)), the median value of a baby boomer portfolio at retirement is $55,000. That is not a lot! Imagine if the boomer lived for another 40 years. It is highly possible. If you are lucky enough to have a sizeable retirement account, then you should try to keep all of that money in it. As I said in previous chapters, it is true that you will have to pay yourself back *with* interest if you borrow from your account, but, in the meantime, you will be losing all kinds of compounding interest that could come in handy during retirement. Another reason to avoid borrowing against your retirement is all of the penalties that you will have to pay. Yeah, they will sock it to ya' if you want that money early. The government gave you a free investment, remember, "pre-tax." Now, they'll want their money at your current tax rate, which is most likely higher than what it will be when you retire. Plus, they'll add an additional penalty to boot! My suggestion is that your retirement account should be a last resort. Counting on it as your emergency fund is not a good idea.

Uncomfortable with Money in the Bank

To be honest, sometimes I am also uncomfortable with *money in the bank*. You build up your emergency fund and the money just sits there. It tempts you. It is easy to get to and there are things that you would like to buy. A new car or TV would be nice. Or maybe even that trip to Cancun. Why can't we just spend this money? Why worry about the future? You can't take it with you when you die, right? No, you can't take it with you but that does not mean you should live irresponsibly nor does it absolve you from being a responsible Christian.

Eventually you will have a car repair, home repair or medical bill and you will be more apt to somehow find the money to pay for the repair than to dip into the emergency fund but the fund is there if you need it.

How Much Do I Need in My Emergency Fund?

Many financial experts will tell you that you should have an emergency fund comprising three to six months of your salary.

Some will tell you that you should have up to a year. Since I talk in net income terms, I suggest enough to cover three to six months of expenses. Based on historical numbers, most people will rarely be unemployed for more than that and most will qualify for unemployment, which will help offset the loss of income.

Our goal is to have money in the bank for a crisis. Imagine having $5,000 or $10,000 or maybe even $20,000 in your bank account. Doesn't it give you a good feeling knowing that you can handle a major bill when it comes your way? I say "when" because it is inevitably going to happen. It is those bills that sink a lot of good people.

When I was a child, I remember a conversation between my mother and my father. My mother's car broke down and they were discussing how it was going to get fixed. It went like this:

"How are we going to pay for it?"

"I don't know. We don't have any money for it."

"What are we going to do? I need my car!"

The questioning went on for a while before turning into accusations, which led to yelling and screaming and eventually to a very unpleasant night of stress for both my mother and father and me. I was probably eight or nine years old at the time and it left a lasting impression on me. Years later, when I got married I told my wife that we would always have $1,000 in the bank. She asked why. I explained that if our car ever needs to be fixed, we're getting it fixed! As I mentioned in the beginning of the book I wanted the fighting to stop. I wanted to learn the lessons from my childhood. Having a mere thousand dollars in the bank helped us tremendously.

Unfortunately, if you are a Bronze or Honorable Mention you will need to wait to start saving for a rainy day. Your number one priority is to pay down your debts and get your day-to-day living expenses under control. Positive cash flow and a lower debt-to-income ratio should be your priority.

Post Tax Investments

A post tax investment is on the other side of a pre-tax investment. The 401(k) deduction gets taken out of your paycheck before taxes are subtracted, hence, a pre-tax investment. A post-tax investment is one that you make after all taxes have been taken out of your pay. It is an investment that you make with your NET income.

If you are at the point where you have your monthly expenses under 65 percent, and you have your emergency/freedom fund at three to six months of your living expenses, then you are ready for some post-tax investing. Congratulations! This is a great place to be. At this point, you can stop putting 15 percent in your emergency/freedom fund and begin using it for post-tax investments.

As I mentioned earlier, it is really up to you to determine what you feel comfortable investing your extra money in. Some people surprise themselves by how much they enjoy investing in real estate. I have had friends swear up and down that they would never invest in real estate when I first met them only to have them follow directly in my investing path. Some even went as far as calling all landlords "slumlords". I do not own "slum" properties nor will I ever manage them in that way. As I've mentioned before, I strive to live all of my life with Colossians 3:23 as my mission statement. I used to get offended but now I just smile because I know it's just a matter of time before they get the same real estate "itch." It's the "unknown" that gets to people—in other words, fear. Don't let fear control your life. Keep the faith and trust in the Lord.

Psalm 20:7

Some trust in chariots and some in horses, but we trust in the name of the LORD our God.

Besides real estate, which I will mention again is *not* for everyone, there are numerous businesses, stocks, bonds and areas in which you can invest your post-tax income. In addition, this extra money can always be given to a good Christian charitable cause. The first step is to pray about it. With that said, let's pray to conclude this chapter.

Dear Lord,

We can't begin to thank You for giving us another chance to be good stewards of Your blessings. We could spend all day naming every detail of our lives where You are present and continually bless us. Please forgive us for living for the world and not completely for You. We pray, Lord, that You enable us to pay our bills, stick to Your plans, save for emergencies and invest wisely. Lord, we know You are always in control and we thank You.

In Jesus' name,
Amen

Chapter X
Spending Your 10% –
Spend it any way you want;
just DON'T create more bad debt

Regardless of where you stand on the podium, there is a bright spot in this plan. You get 10 percent to spend for whatever you want. There are some limitations but this is an exercise we really need. We need to be able to spend without guilt but *with* limits. We need to keep our cash flow in mind and we need to pray before we buy. Pray before we buy? Yes. Let's pray before we begin this chapter.

Oh God,

How we need You! We need You in every tiny detail of our lives. We need You to guide us when we are lost and carry us when we are weary. Lord, at times it seems like You have given us too much freedom to choose. Thank You for Your grace and softening our heart to accept Jesus as our Savior. Thank You for being ever present in our lives. Please open our eyes, ears, hearts and minds to know You are with us. Lord, as we make purchases that are needs as well as wants, please be with us and give us the wisdom to choose wisely.

We are forever in Your debt,
Amen

I mentioned earlier that my spending was like the waves of the ocean. I would be good for a while, then the wave would come crashing down and I would buy something big to make up for all of my goodness. I was "penny-wise, dollar-dumb" as some may put it. I would be good at packing a lunch and not spending on frivolous little things, but then after about a month of that I would go and buy a new guitar amp for $1,000 or maybe even a car! Ah, that doesn't sit well with this plan or any plan for that matter. It is just another reminder that I am not perfect and that I cannot do this by myself. We all need God's hand in our lives…in all areas.

One of my biggest pet peeves is dishonesty. I mean, it is one thing to lie to others but to lie to yourself is terrible. That is why I called for honesty from the beginning of Chapter I. If we can't be honest about where we are right now then we will have no way of getting to a better place later. We need to know our starting point. I will be honest with you right now at this moment. I still struggle with the ebb and flow of my finances. I still wrestle with the wants of this world. I wish I could tell you that it will be easy but I would be telling a lie. It will be hard and it will take discipline. There will be times when you want to buy something but don't have the money for it. You will be tempted to put the charge on the credit card and you will! I still do at times but do not lose hope. Like anything else if we stick with it these times will become less and less frequent.

Pray

I mentioned that we need to pray before making purchases. It may seem like an odd and unnatural thing to do at times but it is absolutely necessary.

How else will we know what God's plan is unless we take time to talk with Him and listen? The little things need prayer and the more expensive items need extra prayer…maybe, no, definitely, the prayers of others as well. Am I telling you to pray before you buy your morning coffee at Starbucks? Seems strange doesn't it? YES! Talk with God. He will lead your heart. We will never know God's will for our lives unless we take the time to ask and we submit to Him. A part of your prayer could be, "Lord, not *my* will be done, but *your* will."

Mark 14:36

36 "Abba, Father," he said, "everything is possible for you. Take this cup from me. Yet not what I will, but what you will."

Personally, I know that when I fail financially in the hustle and bustle of daily living, it is because I am the one in the driver's seat. We have been given so many gifts and as Christian stewards we need to be responsible with them. Even if your cash flow is low or non-existent, you have much to be thankful for. Take time now to write down 10 things you are thankful for, and thank God for all of these things.

I am thankful for:

1.

2.

3.

4.

5.

6.

7.

8.

9.

10.

How does your list look? Did you include "grace" or "family" or "the green grass" or "the air we breathe" or "a new day to live" or "your church"? I think we could easily fill a whole page of "thank-yous" that don't cost a penny. Maybe there is some truth to the phrase "the best things in life are free."

Creator of Heaven and Earth,

Thank You for all of these things that You have blessed us with. Lord, truly the best things in life are free. Our material possessions do occasionally provide comfort and protection but we know it is fleeting. Lord, teach us and bless us with spiritual gifts so much so that we come to a place in our lives where we desire nothing but to serve You. You tell us in Scripture to ask and it shall be given. Lord, hear our prayers. When we make purchases give us wisdom to make the choice You desire. Lord, not to us, not to us, but to Your name be the glory and the praise.

Amen

Chapter XI
Conclusion

My primary purpose of this book was to give you a simple plan for managing your finances and getting out of debt. The Lord had other plans. Finances are not God's priority; you are. If you take one thing away from this book, my hope is that it is this:

God loves you whether you are rich or poor. He is always with us and is eager to hear your thoughts and concerns.

As a child, I never understood the love that God had for us. That is, I saw the drawings and heard the stories of Jesus with the children, but that was long before my time. It wasn't until my first child was born that it really hit me how much God loves his children. I was in the delivery room with my wife and they handed my son to me for the first time. After a very rough delivery, I looked down at a totally helpless, innocent little baby and felt a love for him that no person or thing could ever erase. Unconditionally, I would always love him. It was at that moment that God spoke to me and said, "Craig, now do you see how much I love you?" Wow, if I felt this way about my new baby then how much God must truly love us, unconditionally. Wow! Thank You Lord for being patient with me and teaching me this lesson!

Now, let's summarize what we've learned in the previous chapters.

Getting Started

If you'll remember, the first thing we learned was how to put a personal financial statement (PFS) together and what it all means. We also learned how to determine our NET worth using the personal financial statement.

The Podium—Where Do You Stand?

Using the PFS, we determined where you currently stand financially. Honesty was and is the key. There are no losers; simply Gold, Silver, Bronze and Honorable Mention. Knowing where we currently stand in our finances gives us a starting point so that we can correct what's wrong and take the road to a better place. A key point was tithing. Regardless of where you stand on the podium, you must be a cheerful (not fearful) giver to your church. Remember you don't get to the top of the staircase in one step. We need to take one step at a time. That is, one "podium" rung at a time.

Income—What's Coming In

We all know that when you get a paycheck for doing your job that it is considered your income. We looked at the different types of income, specifically, earned versus passive.

We also looked at some options for increasing your income by investing in businesses (others or your own) and real estate. I gave you my definition of "retirement" and what it means to me.

Remember, retirement doesn't mean your life is over and that you are on the final chapter of your life. It just means a new chapter has begun. Retirement means you now have freedom from your debtors and a tremendous opportunity to serve the Lord. Remember, we are working for the Lord, not men (Colossians 3:23).

Expenses—What's Going Out

One way to increase our income is by eliminating the bills that we have. Before we can do that, we need to know exactly what bills we are paying. We analyzed our expenses and noted the difference between "good debt" and "bad debt." Remember, good debt is debt that makes you money. Bad debt is debt that costs you, each and every month. It is our goal to get rid of all bad debt. When we do this, we increase our cash flow. Cash flow is the money you have remaining at the end of the month after all the bills have been paid. Income minus expenses equals cash flow.

The KO Debt Plan

A simple way to increase your cash flow is by using the Knock Out (KO) Plan. I say "simple" but that doesn't mean it is not painful at times.

It takes discipline to stop spending, which is essential if you want to be successful in getting out of debt. You will forever be on a perpetual spinning cycle much like a gerbil on a wheel if you do not stop spending. The gerbils go and go and go but get nowhere. The plan is simple. It takes the smallest debt you have, pays it off first and then uses that money to pay the next debt off and so on and so forth. By the end, you will have a good chunk of cash flow that you can use for your emergency/freedom fund.

The 65/35 Plan of Action

Most people want a concrete example of how to manage their money. I provided a basic plan for allocating your NET income.

I don't believe you need to micromanage your budget. It is too time consuming and anything time consuming usually gets laid to the wayside. I am not a micro budget kind of guy, but I do believe you need a basic framework for managing your daily finances. To summarize, the 65 percent should cover all of your "necessary" living expenses. The next 10 percent is for tithing. The remaining 15 percent and 10 percent are to be allocated for your emergency/freedom fund and your spending money, respectively. Spending money might not be available if you cash flow is zero or negative.

Living on 65% of Your NET Income

Most of the time, I am not your real estate agent or loan officer's favorite person. Contrary to their opinions, I am a NET guy. I deal in NET numbers, not GROSS. You live off your NET income, not GROSS. So, in my opinion, you should base everything on the NET. Real estate agents and banks want you to borrow as much as possible using your GROSS income. A downturn in the economic climate will reveal who has over extended themselves fairly quickly. Don't buy into it. Prayerfully consider using your NET income.

In this chapter, we also revisited ways to invest in your retirement. The 401(k) is the easiest and seemingly safest way to put money away for the future. The money is taken from your paycheck before it is taxed. So you save from paying taxes and you have more money invested. Most employers also match your contribution, which is another benefit that you should take advantage of.

Investing 10% in Your Spiritual Life

We can do nothing to add to this world or take away from it. God created everything in Heaven and Earth. Man has done a good job of forming what He created into some very cool things. Think of some of the latest technological advances. Wow! We have come a long way. Regardless, we still can't build a ladder to Heaven. The only way to Heaven is through a personal relationship with Jesus Christ. We can't buy God's favor and we shouldn't expect to receive two fold back based on what we give. God calls us to be cheerful givers. (Have I said that yet?) When we give to the Lord, we do it as an act of faith that all things come from Him; the beginning and the end.

The Emergency/Freedom Fund

While many experts will tell you to save three to six months of income for an emergency, I differ slightly. My philosophy is to save three to six months of *expenses*. Much like using NET income to base your finances on, I recommend using "real" numbers for the expenses as well. Having any kind of savings account to be used for emergencies is a good thing. Determining what feels most comfortable to you is something you will need to wrestle with. I am personally content with just three months of reserves. I would not recommend you have less than that. At the other extreme, I have friends that need a whole year's worth to feel safe and secure. How much faith do you have?

Once you have your desired emergency/freedom fund you can use this 15 percent for post-tax investments, such as real estate, businesses or stock/bonds. As I mentioned in this chapter, these types of investments are not for everyone. That doesn't mean you shouldn't step out of your comfort zone. Before you do, talk with others who have invested similarly, learn all you can about it so that you are prepared and, most important, pray for guidance and wisdom.

Spending Money

The final 10 percent in the 65/35 plan is for spending money. Based on where you stand on the podium you may not have any money remaining for spending. You may have already spent it and might still be paying for it on a credit card. If that's the case then *not* spending and paying down your debt is your priority. If you are fortunate enough to have this 10 percent to spend, then spend it wisely. Pray before purchases and pay in cash. Be careful not to create long-term debts with this money.

In Conclusion

It has been my great pleasure writing this book. I hope that it is helpful for you in your daily walk with the Lord. I encourage you to re-read it and pass it on to your friends who may be struggling financially. The bottom line is that regardless of your income, finances - like everything else, is a condition of your heart. If you feel a void in your heart, chances are you will seek to fill it. My prayer for you is that you will trust in the Lord and look to Him for all of your needs—spiritual and financial.

Blessings,
Craig

About the author

Craig Kelley resides in Carlisle, Pennsylvania, and is married to his high school sweetheart, Andrea. They have been married for 17 years and have four beautiful children. They are actively involved in their church, where Craig leads worship services and Bible study. As a schooled musician, he has released four contemporary Christian music CDs. In the business world, Craig has been a part of several start-up companies most notably, Virtual Domains & Servers, Inc., in which he is still at the helm as president and CEO. His primary investments include businesses, rental properties and stocks. Craig enjoys spending time with his family and friends, writing, composing songs and recording them, restoring homes, playing ice hockey and most importantly serving a risen Savior.

Acknowledgements

I am extremely grateful to the many people who have helped me complete this book. It was a fun, frustrating and great learning experience and I couldn't have done it without you. First off, my wife and children, you give me a reason to work hard every day. You bring great joy to my life and your encouragement never goes unnoticed. My friend and spiritual advisor, Sr. Pastor Shad Baker -- your involvement helped take this book to a new level. Thank you for so much of your time and prayers! I would also like to thank Kimberly Largent-Christopher for sharing her expertise in the industry and for her excellent copy-editing skills. Thank you to Jeremy Fallinger for putting up with dozens of changes to the graphics and for the super job he did with them. And finally, I would like to thank God for giving me this opportunity to share what I have learned with others.

Appendix A

To view printable copies please visit http://CactusHillBooks.com.

Asset Sheet

Asset Name	Value (if sold today)	Loan Balance	Monthly Payment
Total:			

Liabilty Sheet

Liability Name	Loan Balance	Monthly Payment
Total:		

Income Sheet

Income Source	Monthy *(NET)*	Yearly *(NET)*
Total:		

Expense Sheet

Expense	Monthy	Yearly
Total:		

Appendix B – IRS – Topic 400 Types of Income

Reference: http://www.irs.gov/taxtopics/tc400.html

1. Wages and Salaries – Topic 401
2. Tips Topic – 402
3. Interest Received – Topic 403
4. Dividends – Topic 404
5. Refunds of State and Local Taxes – Topic 405
6. Alimony Received – Topic 406
7. Business Income – Topic 407
8. Sole Proprietorship – Topic 408
9. Capital Gains and Losses – Topic 409
10. Pensions and Annuities – Topic 410
11. Pensions – The General Rule and the Simplified Method – Topic 411
12. Lump-Sum Distributions – Topic 412
13. Rollovers from Retirement Plans – Topic 413
14. Rental Income and Expenses – Topic 414
15. Renting Residential and Vacation Property (formerly Renting Vacation Property and Renting to Relatives) – Topic 415

Appendix C

Instant company, Crocs edition

How a stay-at-home mom accidentally built and sold a company for $10 million.

By Diane Anderson, Busines 2.0 Magazine
November 2 2006: 6:36 PM EST

(Business 2.0 Magazine) -- How did a stay-at-home mom start a business that she later sold to Crocs for $10 million? "It was an accident," says Sheri Schmelzer, 41, of Boulder, Colo.

One day in summer 2005, she decided to use clay and rhinestones to make charms that would fit snugly into the holes of her family's 10 pairs of Crocs. When husband Rich came home, he saw the potential.

There are 26 million pairs of Crocs in the world, more than 80 percent of them speckled by holes, and many of those shoes are on the feet of accessory-friendly youth. Jibbitz, as the charms (and the company) came to be known, can be anything - peace signs, flowers, you name it - to please a demographic eager for variety.

Within weeks, the Schmelzers set up a website for sales. By the end of the summer, they were funded by home equity, with their parents working the assembly line in the basement.

Jibbitz isn't just a family-business fairy tale: It's a study in piggybacking on a product phenomenon.

In February, when the company sold its 250,000th piece, Jibbitz products were carried in 300 stores and pulled in $212,000 in sales; 6 million pieces of Jibbitz later, in August, the products were in 3,000 stores and garnered sales of $2.2 million.

The Schmelzers outsourced manufacturing to Asia and stepped up to a 12,000-square-foot office and warehouse in Boulder. In October the Schmelzers agreed to take $10 million from Crocs for the company, which will operate as a subsidiary, plus $10 million more if they hit earnings targets.

APPENDIX D

Figure 1 - Bad Debt That We Are Going to KO!

Description	Monthy Minimum Payment	Balance
1.		
2.		
3.		
4.		
5.		
6.		
7.		
8.		
9.		
10.		
11.		
12.		
13.		
14.		

APPENDIX E

The following chart shows what the bank says your maximum monthly payment and maxium allowable debt load could be, based on your gross (pre-tax) annual income:

Bank debt-to-income ratio examples		
Gross income	**28% of monthly**	**36% of monthly**
$20,000	$467	$600
$30,000	$700	$900
$40,000	$933	$1,200
$50,000	$1,167	$1,500
$60,000	$1,400	$1,800
$80,000	$1,867	$2,400
$100,000	$2,333	$3,000
$150,000	$3,500	$4,500

APPENDIX F

The monkey likes his veggies, syringes

January 14, 2007

BY DAVID ROEDER Sun-Times Columnist

This year, **Mr. Adam Monk,** the Sun-Times' stock-picking monkey who has beaten the market for four years running, is into erectile dysfunction. He's also into syringes, women's clothes and fresh fruit and vegetables. But don't get the wrong idea.

These are the businesses of Mr. Monk's latest stock picks, made last week exclusively for the Sun-Times. And that means only one thing: It's time again for the Sun-Times Monkey Manager stock-picking contest, celebrating the wisdom of the everyday investor and primate.

Yes, despite all you hear about consolidation and cost-cutting in the Mainstream Media, with its Incredible Shrinking Newspapers, here we are back with the contest this year, and again with a fabulous prize for the reader who guesses the top-gaining stock of 2007. It's from **Apple Vacations, America's Favorite Vacation Company,** and details run alongside this story.

To get the stock-guessing juices flowing, I visited Mr. Monk last week at his natural habitat, **Animal Rentals Inc.,** 5742 W. Grand. The senior-citizen cebus monkey crawled over newspaper stock pages (yes, we found some!) arrayed on a desk, and marked his five favorites with a pen. It's now a time-honored ritual, documented by a Sun-Times photographer and the accounting firm Howard, Fine & Howard.

In the four years since Mr. Monk, wearing an NFL shirt in support of the Bears, has chaired and inspired the Sun-Times stock-picking contest, his stocks have posted annual returns that beat the major indexes each time.

(Rich Hein/Sun-Times)

His selections are included in an accompanying table. Sharp-eyed readers will notice that Mr. Monk, progressive as ever, is trying something new. One of his stocks isn't a stock at all, strictly speaking. It's an exchange-traded fund, **Market 2000 HOLDRS Trust (MKH),** which represents shares of the 50 largest-cap companies.

"It's going to be a big year for that part of the market," Mr. Monk told this reporter. "I had this pathetic intern working for me, and I told him to go buy me some large caps. He came back with this boxload of incredibly ugly cheesehead things. So I got into that market with this ETF."

His other picks include companies in pharmaceutical supplies (the syringes) and medical devices (for sundry pelvic issues), historically two of Mr. Monk's favorite sectors. Rounding out his portfolio are **Fresh Del Monte Produce Inc. (FDP)** and ladies' apparel maker **Cygne Designs Inc. (CYDS).**

The latter two stocks had really bad years in 2006, but Mr. Monk insisted they are bouncing back. "Any monkey knows you can't go wrong with bananas and pineapples," he said. "Cygne makes jeans and skimpy tops for teenagers. Believe me, it's not spending much on material."

Mr. Monk invited readers to follow his stocks all year, with updates in the Sun-Times and at *www.sun times.com,* and to top his performance by submitting a stock for the contest.

In the four years since Mr. Monk has chaired and inspired this contest, his stocks have posted annual returns of 37 percent, 36 percent, 3 percent and, in 2006, 36 percent, beating the major indexes every time. It's proof that you don't have to be an insider CEO, an insider hedge-fund manager or a loudmouth on CNBC to make money in the market.

Our readers have responded to his example with stock picks that gained 100 percent, 200 percent and way higher. So take your best shot again this year.

Mr. Monk is with you all the way, while also tending to his latest venture, as previously reported. He has founded a company to produce the next generation in camera-, phone-, Internet-, music- and game-linked devices that will provide you with every technological convenience while recording your every move to build the most massive consumer database known to man. It is nothing less than a campaign for global domination.

It's called **Private Eye Electronic Products (PEEP)** and Mr. Monk gave me the latest update.

"We're going after Steve Jobs with our new device, the iPEEP. We're also launching our version of the BlackBerry, only it will be for the late adopters of technology. We call it the ElderBerry. And I have responded to

227

the City of Chicago's call for proposals on offering free Wi-Fi access to everybody." That sounds exciting, I said.

Mr. Monk hesitated. "I'm not too sure about the city," he said. "I went to my alderman and said I want to offer free Wi-Fi. My alderman -- he's up there in years a bit -- said, 'Whaa . . . you want a free hi-fi?' Trust me, there's a steep learning curve with the city on this whole thing."

I told Mr. Monk that I was amazed by his new ideas and ventures. Why, I asked, does he do this when, at age 35, he's geriatric for a cebus monkey and could retire on all the laurels and riches he's gained for his stock expertise?

"It's all a matter of challenging yourself," he said, "and of taking what's out there and improving it. For example, there's Donald Trump and his show, 'The Apprentice.' That whole franchise is obviously failing. So I've signed as senior producer of a new show where people compete to serve my organization and replace that pathetic intern who bought the cheeseheads. I call the show 'The Pathetic Interns.' And you'll love my twist on the concept."

What's the twist?

"I signed that Hilton woman to star in it. She'll lord it over the contestants in a vaguely dominatrix sort of way."

Imagine that, I said. You signed Paris Hilton?

"No, no. She's got a sister, a real up-and-comer. Stockholm Hilton. She got the brain genes in the family."

What channel will carry the show?

"For Mr. Monk, there's only one. Animal Planet."

72927323R00128

Made in the USA
Middletown, DE
09 May 2018